Complete Study Edition

Othello

| Commentary | Complete Text | Glossary |

edited by

JAMES K. LOWERS

Professor of English
University of Hawaii

Cliff's Notes
INCORPORATED

LINCOLN, NEBRASKA 68501

ISBN 0-8220-1434-3

Copyright © 1968, 1966
by
Cliffs Notes, Inc.

Originally published under the
title "Othello: Complete Study
Guide," copyright © 1966.

Othello

SHAKESPEARE WAS NEVER MORE MEANINGFUL—

. . . than when read in Cliff's "Complete Study Edition." The introductory sections give you all of the background information about the author and his work necessary for reading with understanding and appreciation. A descriptive bibliography provides guidance in the selection of works for further study. The inviting three-column arrangement of the complete text offers the maximum in convenience to the reader. Adjacent to the text there is a running commentary that provides clear supplementary discussion of the play as it develops. Obscure words and obsolete usages used by Shakespeare are explained in the glosses directly opposite to the line in which they occur. The numerous allusions are also clarified.

JAMES K. LOWERS—

. . . the editor of this Shakespeare "Complete Study Edition" was graduated from the University of California at Los Angeles. Subsequently, he obtained his masters and doctoral degrees at the same institution. He taught for a year at Chico State College, Chico, California, and at UCLA for nine years. Since 1951, Dr. Lowers has been a member of the faculty at the University of Hawaii, where he is now a professor of English.

Othello

Contents

The Tragedy
of
Othello

hath bene sundry times publiquely :
right Honourable the Lord Cham
his Seruants.

THE MOST EX:
cellent and lamentable
Tragedie, of Romeo
and *Iuliet.*

an introduction

THE
Tragicall Historie of
HAMLET,
Prince of Denmarke.

By William Shakespeare.

Newly imprinted and enlarged to almost as much
againe as it was, according to the true and perfect
Coppie.

AT LONDON.
Printed by I. R. for N. L. and are to be sold at his
shoppe vnder Saint Dunstons Church in.

Two books are essential to the library of any English-speaking household; one of these is the Bible and the other is the works of William Shakespeare. These books form part of the house furnishings, not as reading material generally, but as the symbols of religion and culture—sort of a twentieth-century counterpart of the ancient Roman household gods. This symbolic status has done a great deal of damage both to religion and to Shakespeare.

Whatever Shakespeare may have been, he was not a deity. He was a writer of popular plays, who made a good living, bought a farm in the country, and retired at the age of about forty-five to enjoy his profits as a gentleman. The difference between Shakespeare and the other popular playwrights of his time was that he wrote better plays —plays that had such strong artistic value that they have been popular ever since. Indeed, even today, if Shakespeare could col-

2

William to Shakespeare.

lect his royalties, he would be among the most prosperous of playwrights.

During the eighteenth century but mostly in the nineteenth, Shakespeare's works became "immortal classics," and the cult of Shakespeare-worship was inaugurated. The plays were largely removed from their proper place on the stage into the library where they became works of literature rather than drama and were regarded as long poems, attracting all the artistic and psuedo-artistic atmosphere surrounding poetry. In the nineteenth century this attitude was friendly but later, and especially in the early twentieth century, a strange feeling arose in the English-speaking world that poetry was sissy stuff, not for men but for "pansies" and women's clubs. This of course is sheer nonsense.

This outline will present a detailed analysis of the play and background information which will show the play in its proper perspective. This means seeing the play in relation to the other plays, to the history of the times when they were written, and in relation to the theatrical technique required for their successful performance.

G. B. Harrison's book *Introducing Shakespeare,* published by Penguin Books, will be of value for general information about Shakespeare and his plays. For reference material on the Elizabethan Theater, consult E. K. Chambers, *The Elizabethan Theatre* (four volumes). For study of the organization and production methods of this theater see *Henslowe's Diary* edited by W. W. Greg. Again for general reading the student will enjoy Margaret Webster's *Shakespeare Without Tears,* published by Whittlesey House (McGraw-Hill) in 1942.

The remainder of the Introduction will be divided into sections discussing Shakespeare's life, his plays, and his theater.

LIFE OF WILLIAM SHAKESPEARE

From the standpoint of one whose main interest lies with the plays themselves, knowledge of Shakespeare's life is not very important. Inasmuch as it treats of the period between 1592 and 1611, when the plays were being written, knowledge of his life is useful in that it may give some clues as to the topical matters introduced into the plays. For instance, the scene of Hamlet's advice to the players (Act III Scene ii) takes on an added significance when considered along with the fame and bombastic style of Edward Alleyn, the then famous actor-manager of the Lord Admiral's Players (the most powerful rivals of Shakespeare's company).

This biography is pieced together from the surviving public records of the day, from contemporary references in print, and from the London Stationer's Register. It is by no means complete. The skeletal nature of the biographical material available to scholars has led commentators in the past to invent part of the story to fill it out. These parts have frequently been invented by men who were more interested in upholding a private theory than in telling the truth, and this habit of romancing has led to a tradition of inaccurate Shakespearian biography. For this reason this outline may be of use in disposing of bad traditions.

In the heyday of the self-made man, the story developed that Shakespeare was a poor boy from the village, virtually uneducated, who fled from Stratford to London to escape prosecution for poaching on the lands of Sir Thomas Lucy, and there by his talent and a commendable industry raised himself to greatness. This rags-to-riches romance was in the best Horatio Alger tradition but was emphatically not true. The town records of Stratford make it clear that John Shakespeare, father of the playwright, was far from a pauper. He was a wealthy and responsible citizen who held in turn several municipal offices. He married (1557) Mary Arden, the daughter of a distinguished Catholic family. William, their third son, was baptized in the Parish Church in 1564. He had a good grammar school education. Ben Jonson's remark that Shakespeare had "small Latin and less Greek" did not mean the same in those days, when the educated man had a fluent command of

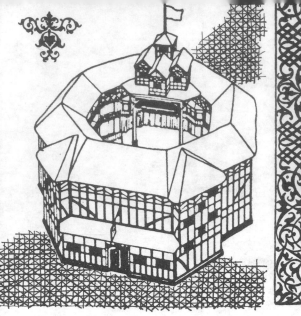

Exterior view of "The Globe"

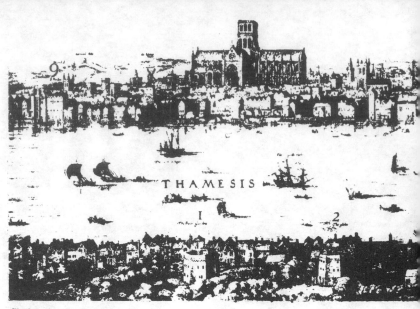

Shakespeare's London

Interior view of "The Globe"

an introduction to Shakespeare

Latin and probably at least a reading knowledge of Greek, as it does now when classical scholars are few. The remark has been construed by the Horatio Alger people as meaning that Shakespeare reached London a semi-literate bumpkin; it is nonsense. It means merely that Shakespeare was not a university man, as most of the writers were, and that the University Wits were taking out their jealousy in snobbery and pointing out that Shakespeare used less purely literary symbolism than they did.

Shakespeare married Ann Hathaway when he was eighteen years old. She was some years older than he and the marriage seems to have been a rather hasty affair. Five months after the marriage, Suzanna, the first child, was born. Two years later, in 1585, twins Hamnet and Judith were baptized.

No one knows when Shakespeare came to London. The first mention of him occurs in the bad-tempered pamphlet which Robert Greene, one of the University Wits and a famous playwright, wrote just before his death. Greene complains of "an upstart crow, beautified with our feathers, that with his tiger's heart wrapped in a player's hide, supposes he is as well able to bombast out a blank verse as the best of you; and being an absolute Yohannes factotum, is in his own conceit the only Shakescene in a country." This was written in 1592 and indicates not only that Shakespeare was in London at the time, but that he was writing plays and beginning to make such a name for himself as to call forth the jealous apprehension of an established writer.

The next year, 1593, was a year of plague, and by order of the Lord Mayor and the Aldermen, the theaters were closed. The players, disorganized by this action, went on tour outside of London. During this year Shakespeare's two long poems, *Venus and Adonis* and *The Rape of Lucrece,* were entered in the Stationer's Register. Both were dedicated to the Earl of Southampton.

The public theaters had not been established very long. The first of these, called the Theatre, was built for James Burbage in 1576. By 1594, there were three such theaters in London, the two new houses being the Curtain and the Rose. By 1594, also, the three most celebrated of the writers, Kyd, Greene, and Marlowe were dead, and Shakespeare had already a considerable reputation. Before this date the theaters had been largely low class entertainment and the plays had been of rather poor quality. Through the revival of classical drama in the schools (comedies) and the Inns of Court (tragedies), an interest had been created in the stage. The noblemen of the time were beginning to attend the public theaters, and their tastes demanded a better class of play.

Against the background of this

increasing status and upper-class popularity of the theaters, Shakespeare's company was formed. After the 1594 productions under Alleyn, this group of actors divided. Alleyn formed a company called the Lord Admiral's Company which played in Henslowe's Rose Theatre. Under the leadership of the Burbages (James was the owner of the Theatre and his son Richard was a young tragic actor of great promise), Will Kemp (the famous comedian), and William Shakespeare, the Lord Chamberlain's company came into being. This company continued throughout Shakespeare's career. It was renamed in 1603, shortly after Queen Elizabeth's death, becoming the King's players.

The company played at the Theatre until Burbage's lease on the land ran out. The landlord was not willing to come to satisfactory terms. The company moved across the river and built the new Globe theater. The principal sharers in the new place were Richard and Cuthbert Burbage each with two and a half shares and William Shakespeare, John Heminge, Angustus Phillips, Thomas Pope, and Will Kemp, each with one share.

Burbage had wanted to establish a private theater and had rented the refectory of the old Blackfriars' monastery. Not being allowed to use this building he leased it to a man called Evans who obtained permission to produce plays acted by chil-dren. This venture was so successful as to make keen competition for the existing companies. This vogue of child actors is referred to in *Hamlet*, Act II Scene ii.

The children continued to play at Blackfriars until, in 1608, their license was suspended because of the seditious nature of one of their productions. By this time the public attitude towards the theaters had changed, and Burbage's Company, now the King's players, could move into the Blackfriars theater.

Partners with the Burbages in this enterprise were Shakespeare, Heminge, Condell, Sly, and Evans. This was an indoor theater, whereas the Globe had been outdoors. The stage conditions were thus radically altered. More scenery could be used; lighting effects were possible. Shakespeare's works written for this theater show the influence of change in conditions.

To return to the family affairs of the Shakespeares, records show that in 1596 John Shakespeare was granted a coat of arms and, along with his son, was entitled to call himself "gentleman." In this year also, William Shakespeare's son Hamnet died. In 1597 William Shakespeare bought from William Underwood a sizable estate at Stratford, called New Place.

Shakespeare's father died in 1601, his mother, in 1608. Both of his daughters married, one in 1607, the other in 1616.

During this time, Shakespeare went on acquiring property in Stratford. He retired to New Place probably around 1610 although this date is not definitely established, and his career as a dramatist was practically at an end. *The Tempest,* his last complete play, was written around the year 1611.

The famous will, in which he left his second best bed to his wife, was executed in 1616 and later on in that same year he was buried.

THE PLAYS

Thirty-seven plays are customarily included in the works of William Shakespeare. Scholars have been at great pains to establish the order in which these plays were written. The most important sources of information for this study are the various records of performances which exist, the printed editions which came out during Shakespeare's career, and such unmistakable references to current events as may crop up in the plays. The effect of the information gathered in this way is generally to establish two dates between which a given play must have been written. In *Hamlet* for instance, there is a scene in which Hamlet refers to the severe competition given to the adult actors by the vogue for children's performances. This vogue first became a serious threat to the professional companies in about 1600. In 1603 a very bad edition was published, without authorization, of *The*

Elizabethan types

Lute, standing cup, stoop

Queen Elizabeth

an introduction to Shakespeare

Tragical History of Hamlet, Prince of Denmark by William Shakespeare. These two facts indicate that *Hamlet* was written between the years of 1600 and 1603. This process fixed the order in which most of the plays were written. Those others of which no satisfactory record could be found were inserted in their logical place in the series according to the noticeable development of Shakespeare's style. In these various ways we have arrived at the following chronological listing of the plays.

1591 *Henry VI Part I*
Henry VI Part II
Henry VI Part III
Richard III
Titus Andronicus
Love's Labour Lost
The Two Gentlemen of Verona
The Comedy of Errors
The Taming of the Shrew

1594 *Romeo and Juliet*
A Midsummer Night's Dream
Richard II
King John
The Merchant of Venice

1597 *Henry IV Part I*
Henry IV Part II
Much Ado About Nothing
Merry Wives of Windsor
As You Like It
Julius Caesar
Henry V
Troilus and Cressida

1601 *Hamlet*
Twelfth Night
Measure for Measure
All's Well That Ends Well

Othello

1606 *King Lear*
Macbeth
Timon of Athens
Antony and Cleopatra
Coriolanus

1609 *Pericles*

1611 *Cymbeline*
The Winter's Tale
The Tempest
Henry VIII

At this point it is pertinent to review the tradition of dramatic form that had been established before Shakespeare began writing. Drama in England sprang at the outset from the miracle and morality plays of the medieval guilds. These dramatized Bible stories became increasingly less religious as time passed until finally they fell into disrepute. The next development was the writing of so-called *interludes*. These varied in character but often took the form of bawdy farce. As the renaissance gathered force in England, Roman drama began to be revived at the schools and the Inns of Court. Before long English writers were borrowing plots and conventions wholesale from the classic drama. The Italian model was the most fashionable and consequently was largely adopted, but many features of the old *interludes* still persisted, especially in plays written for the public theaters.

With the development among the nobility of a taste for the theater, a higher quality of work became in demand. Very few of

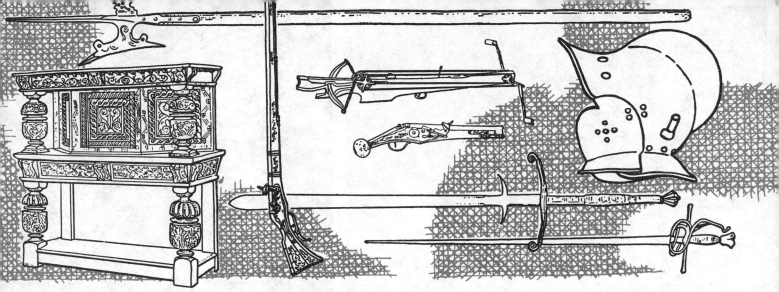

Court cupboard, crossbow, guns, sword, rapier, halberd, burgonet

the very early plays have survived. The reason for this is that the plays were not printed to be read; no one considered them worth the trouble. A play was strung together out of a set of stock characters and situations with frantic haste, often by as many as a dozen different men. These men who worked on plays did not regard their writing activity as of prime importance. They were primarily actors. With the cultivation of taste for better plays came the idea that the work of a playwright was an effort demanding special skill. The highborn audiences were interested in the plays themselves and began to include editions of their favorite plays in their libraries. With this demand for printed copies of the plays, the conception began of the dramatist as an artist in his own right, whether or not he acted himself (as most of them did).

By 1592, when Shakespeare began to make his personal reputation, a set of traditions had developed. This body of traditions gave Shakespeare the basic materials with which to work.

A special type of comedy writing had developed, centered around the name of John Lyly, designed for the sophisticated audience of the court and presented with lavish dances and decorative effects. This type of play was characterized by a delicately patterned artificiality of speech. The dialogue was studded with complicated references to Latin and Italian literature that the renaissance had made fashionable.

Shakespeare used this method extensively. In the early plays (before *The Merchant of Venice*) he was experimenting and wrote much that is nothing more than conventional. Later on, as his mature style developed, the writing becomes integral with and indispensable to the play and no longer appears artificial. In *Romeo and Juliet*, an early play, the following lines are spoken by Lady Capulet in urging Juliet to accept the Count Paris for her husband. These lines are brilliant but artificial, and the play seems to pause in order that this trick bit of word-acrobatics may be spoken.

> Read o'er the volume of young Paris' face,
> And find delight, writ there with beauty's pen.
> Examine every married lineament,
> And see how one another lends content:
> And what obscured in this fair volume lies,
> Find written in the margent of his eyes.
> This precious book of love, this unbound lover,
> To beautify him only needs a cover!

The other most important dramatic tradition was that of tragedy. The Elizabethan audiences liked spectacular scenes; they also had a great relish for scenes of sheer horror. This led to a school of tragic writing made popular by Kyd and Marlowe.

These plays were full of action and color and incredible wickedness, and the stage literally ran with artificial blood. Shakespeare's early tragedies are directly in this tradition, but later the convention becomes altered and improved in practice, just as that of comedy had done. The scene in *King Lear* where Gloucester has his eyes torn out stems from this convention. Lear, however, is a comparatively late play and the introduction of this scene does not distort or interrupt its organization.

Shakespeare's stylistic development falls into a quite well-defined progression. At first he wrote plays according to the habit of his rivals. He very quickly began experimenting with his technique. His main concern seems to be with tricks of language. He was finding out just what he could do. These early plays use a great deal of rhyme, seemingly just because Shakespeare liked writing rhyme. Later on, rhyme is used only when there is a quite definite dramatic purpose to justify it. Between the early plays and those which may be called mature (*The Merchant of Venice* is the first of the mature plays), there is a basic change in method. In the early works Shakespeare was taking his patterns from previous plays and writing his own pieces, quite consciously incorporating one device here and another there.

In the later period these tricks of the trade had been tested and

7

The world as known in 1600

Elizabethan coins

absorbed; they had become not contrived methods but part of Shakespeare's mind. This meant that, quite unconsciously, while his total attention was focused on the emotional and intellectual business of writing a masterpiece, he wrote in terms of the traditional habits he had learned and used in the earlier period. (*Henry IV, Julius Caesar, Henry V,* and *Hamlet* are the plays of this advanced stage.)

The group of plays between 1606 and 1609 shows a further new development. Having reached mastery of his medium in terms of dramatic technique (with *Othello*) and of power over the tension of thought in moving easily through scenes of comedy, pathos, and tragedy, he turned again to the actual literary quality of his plays and began to enlarge his scope quite beyond and apart from the theatrical traditions of his day. The early results of this new attempt are the two plays *King Lear* and *Macbeth.* The change in these plays is in the direction of concentration of thought. The attempt is, by using masses of images piled one on another, to convey shadings and intensities of emotion not before possible. He was trying to express the inexpressible. For example the following is from the last part of

an introduction
to Shakespeare

Lady Macbeth's famous speech in Act I, Scene v:

Come, thick night,
And pall thee in the dunnest smoke of hell,
That my keen knife see not the wound it makes,
Nor heaven peep through the blanket of the dark,
To cry, hold, hold!

Compare the concentrated imagery of this speech with Hamlet's soliloquy at the end of Act III, Scene ii.

'Tis now the very witching time of night,
When churchyards yawn, and hell itself breathes out
Contagion to this world: now could I drink hot blood,
And do such bitterness as the day
Would quake to look on.

The sentiment of these two speeches is similar, but the difference in method is striking and produces a difference again in the type of effect. The *Lear-Macbeth* type of writing produces a higher tension of subtlety but tends to collect in masses rather than to move in lines as the lighter, more transparent writing of *Hamlet* does.

Shakespeare's last plays were conceived for the new indoor theater at Blackfriars and show this is in a more sophisticated type of staging. In *The Tempest,* last and most celebrated of these late comedies, there is dancing, and much complicated staging (such as the disappearing banquet, the ship at sea, and so on). The writing of plays for the

more distinguished audience of Blackfriars, and the increased stage resources there provided, influenced the form of the plays.

The writing of these plays forms a culmination. In his early apprenticeship Shakespeare had been extravagant in word-acrobatics, testing the limits of his technique. In the Lear-Macbeth period of innovation he had tried the limits of concentrated emotion to the point almost of weakening the dramatic effectiveness of the plays. In *The Tempest* his lines are shaken out into motion again. He seems to have been able to achieve the subtlety he was after in verse of light texture and easy movement, no longer showing the tendency to heaviness or opacity visible in *King Lear* and *Macbeth.*

THE THEATER

The first public theater in London was built in the year 1576 for James Burbage and was called simply The Theatre. Before this time players' companies had performed for the public in the courtyards of the city inns. For a more select public they frequently played in the great halls of institutions, notably the Inns of Court. The stage and auditorium of the Elizabethan theater were based on these traditions and combined features of both the hall and the inn-yard. The auditorium was small. There was a pit where the orchestra seats would be in a modern playhouse; this section was for the lowest classes who stood during the performances. Around the

8

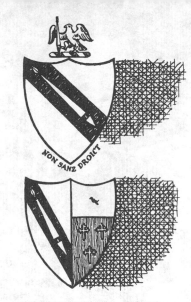

Shakespeare's Coat of Arms

Wood cut camp illustration

wall was a gallery for the gentry. The galleries and the tiring-house behind the fore-stage were roofed; the rest was open to the sky. The stage consisted of a very large platform that jutted out so that the pit audience stood on three sides of it. Behind this, under the continuation behind the stage of the gallery, was the inner stage; this was supplied with a curtain, but the open fore-stage was not. Above this inner stage was a balcony (really a continuation of the gallery), forming still another curtained stage. This gallery was used for kings addressing subjects from balconies, for the storming of walls, for Juliet's balcony and bedroom, for Cleopatra's monument and so on. Costumes and properties were extravagant (such as guillotines, fountains, ladders, etc.); extensive music was constantly used and such sound effects as cannon, drums, or unearthly screams were common; but there was no painted scenery as we know it; there was no darkness to focus attention on the stage, no facilities for stage-lighting. All these things are in marked contrast to the modern stage conventions and thus a serious problem of adaptation is posed when it comes to producing the plays under present day conditions.

The advantages are not all with the modern stage. It is true that the modern or picture stage can do more in the way of realistic effects, but this kind of realism is not important to good drama. In fact there has been a recent trend away from realistic scenery in the theater back to a conventional or stylized simplicity.

One effect of Shakespeare's stage upon his work was to make the scenes in the plays more person-scenes than place-scenes. As a matter of fact in many cases the places assigned in the texts to various scenes were not in the original and have only been added by an editor who did not understand this very fact.

It used to be said that *Antony and Cleopatra* could not be staged and was written to be read rather than acted. The grounds for this statement were that in the fourth act there were no less than fourteen scenes. To some, a scene means a change of place and requires a break in the play while scenery is shifted. To Shakespeare these scenes meant no such thing; they meant, simply, that there were fourteen different groupings of people, successively and without any break, carrying on the action of the play. The scene headings when added should have been (1) Caesar, (2) Antony and Cleopatra, (3) the common soldiers, etc., instead of (1) Before Alexandria, (2) Alexandria, a room in the palace, etc. By this you may see that with all its limitations, the Elizabethan stage had a measure of flexibility that the modern stage could envy.

Fashions in staging Shakespeare have altered radically in the last few years. At the close of the nineteenth century, Sir Herbert Beerbohm Tree staged a spectacular series of pageant productions. All the tricks of romantic realistic staging were used and, if necessary, the play was twisted, battered, and re-written to accommodate the paraphernalia.

The modern method is to produce the plays as nearly according to the text as possible and work out a compromise to achieve the sense of space and of flexibility necessary, yet without departing so far from the stage habits of today as to confuse or divert the audience. This technique was inaugurated by Granville-Barker in the early twentieth century. With the exception of such extravagant stunts as Orson Welles' production of *Julius Caesar* in modern dress (set in Chicago and complete with tommy-guns), the prevailing practice now is to use simple, stylized scenery adapted to the needs of producing the play at full length.

Much can be done in the way of learning Shakespeare through books, but the only sure way is to see a well produced performance by a good company of actors. Whatever genius Shakespeare may have possessed as a psychologist, philosopher, or poet, he was first of all a man of the theater, who knew it from the inside, and who wrote plays so well-plotted for performance that from his day up to the present, no great actor has been able to resist them.

Othello, Desdemona and jealous Iago

an introduction

THE TEXT

Othello, the latest of the Shakespearean quartos, was entered in the Stationers' Register f o r Thomas Walkley under the date October 1, 1621, and was published in the following year. The title page provides evidence that it had been many times acted at the Globe and at Blackfriars. The next appearance of the play was in the First Folio (hereinafter referred to as F₁), where it is listed under the "Tragedies" and occupies pages 310-19. F₁ was entered under the date November 8, 1623, by William Jaggard and Edward Blount and (as the title page tells us) was published in the same year. A third edition of the play, Q₂, was published in 1630. All three editions have differences, chiefly minor, but F₁ gives 160 lines not to be found in Q₁ which even omits that poetical gem, the Pontic Sea simile (III.iii.453-9). Understandably, F₁ is the chief source of the present text. It may be pointed out that it had been "most delicately refined," apparently because of the Parliamentary law prohibiting the use of oaths, especially the use of God's name in stage plays. The editor or editors of Q₁ must be credited with providing stage directions, which in F₁ are not helpful enough for stage presentation. It has been argued that F₁ was set not from a manuscript but from a copy of Q₁ which had been corrected.

THE DATE OF THE PLAY

If one excepts the chronicle historical tragedies, *Richard III* and *Richard II, Othello* ranks as Shakespeare's fourth tragedy, and following *Hamlet,* the second of the great high tragedies which include *King Lear* and *Macbeth.* Scholars have favored a date of composition as early as 1602, especially because in the play appear phrases which could have been borrowed from the First Quarto of *Hamlet,* which was entered in the Stationers' Register in July, 1602; and because of Shakespeare's apparent use of Philemon Holland's translation of Pliny's *Natural History* (1601). Early scholars have favored a date as late as 1612-13 since records tell us that the play was one of fourteen selected in May 1613 for performance at

The Tragedy of Othello

Court. But later there came to light a document held to be part of the official books of Revels (Court entertainments) in which is found a record of a performance of the play at Whitehall in November, 1604. Although the authenticity of this document has been challenged, the consensus now is that it is authentic, or at least a faithful copy of the original. Therefore a large proportion of scholars willingly accept the year 1604 as the correct date of composition. Certainly the stylistic features suggest a date not later than 1606 and possibly as early as 1602. It is enough to say that *Othello* belongs to the third period in Shakspeare's creative life, a period when we see him at the height of his powers.

SOURCE OF PLOT

The Othello story came from that collection long known to Elizabethans, the *Hecatommithi* by Giraldo Cinthio which was first published in Sicily in 1565. The Italian's tale is ostensibly related as a warning to ladies not to marry men of foreign races and strange manners, and Cin-

thio capitalized upon the fact that the cruelty of the Moors was something of a byword during the Renaissance.

The Cinthio story is a bare narration of sordid details completely lacking in power and structure. In it the Moor's ancient (Iago)) is motivated by love for Desdemona. The author does introduce the Cassio episodes which are so important to the play. As in the drama, the one involving the handkerchief convinces the Moor that his wife is unfaithful to him, and he directs the ancient to kill her. He stands by as the young wife is beaten to death with a stocking filled with sand. This crude incident is the climax, but the action does not fall to a catastrophe. Not only does the protagonist screen himself by pulling down a beam from the ceiling and declaring that the death was accidental, but there follows a long sequel involving the torture and banishment of the Moor, his ultimate death at the hands of Desdemona's kin, and the death of the ancient, who had been imprisoned for a wholly unconnected offense.

From the point of Desdemona's death, the action is episodic, lacking the unity which is achieved by closely knitting together the incidents in a cause-and effect relationship. Attention is divided between the fate of the ancient and that of the Moor.

Shakespeare, to be sure, rejected the cruder incidents in this story, but his adaptation actually includes two more that the number found in Cinthio: Roderigo's pursuit of Desdemona and the Cassio-Bianca affair. The first act is entirely original with him. Moreover, he changed Iago's motive and closely related subsidiary actions to the main one. Thus he transmuted dross into gold. *Othello* properly takes its place among the great dramatic tragedies of world literature. Here is a play commendable for its unity of action and tone, its fine emphasis upon a single theme, its vehemence of emotion found in all the major characters. Little wonder that the play has been held to be the most successfully acted of Shakespeare's tragedies.

Jealousy is eating away at Othello

Cassio's mistress rejects handkerchief

SPECIAL PROBLEMS IN OTHELLO

It must be conceded that a few commentators regard *Othello* as a domestic rather than a high tragedy. Of course most of the characters are of lower rank than those found in other Shakespearean high tragedies. Apart from the figure of the Duke, the poet introduces a senator, his daughter, and three army officers. But we shall see, as we follow the text and summary comments, that *Othello* is not just a play at the personal, domestic level — one concerned with the jealous husband; that the hero is elevated to the status worthy of the protagonist in high tragedy; that it involves issues of great public import. One might add parenthetically that the theme of a husband's jealousy is common enough in actual life so that the audiences do achieve a sense of personal involvement — of empathy — more readily than they do with plays involving rulers of kingdoms and heirs

an introduction to the tragedy of Othello

to the Crown. To be able to use this theme and still attain high tragedy is one of the measures of Shakespeare's genius.

One must admit that many commentators have found difficulty relating to the time element in the play. Nor can one deny that a careful reading of the text reveals some inconsistency in this respect. For example, there is absolutely no time for the acts or acts of adultery to have taken place after the arrival in Cyprus, nor has Cassio had time to engage in an affair of any duration with Bianca, the Courtesan. Furthermore, Othello's concern is not that his wife may have had pre-marital experience, but that she has been unfaithful to him after their marriage. In an effort to justify the poet's practice, as early as 1849 a "double time" theory was formulated, one that still recommends itself to many students of the play. But the important thing to remember is that Shakespeare, practical man of the theater, knew exactly what he was doing. Rapidity of movement is desirable if one is to attain dramatic tension and even credibility. For as the plot advances it is touch and go with the villain of the piece, whose plans will fail if there is an appreciable delay. Certainly the author was skillful enough in his handling of the time scheme to make the entire

action seem entirely probable to his audiences.

THE PRINCIPAL CHARACTERS

Othello: As has been indicated above, in Shakespeare's adaptation of Cinthio's story, the Moor is magnified and ennobled; he is, as it were, "larger than life," as are all the dramatist's protagonists in the great tragedies. Othello is not to be measured in terms of the sordid details of the intrigue which culminate in his own death. He towers in sheer force and nobility above all others in Venice throughout the larger part of the play; from first to last he is aware of his high position. For example, in I.iii. he identifies himself with the "great ones" of the world — and he does so without the slightest show of arrogance. Other details in support of this generalization are profuse enough and will be noted in the summaries. If he does embrace evil, falling the victim of the machinations of Iago during the temptation scene (III.iii) and in the so-called "brothel scene" (IV.ii), wherein he publicly denounces his wife, he recovers himself and becomes convinced that he must function as the scourge of God, executing not vengeance but justice upon one who, he is convinced, may contaminate others.

One may legitimately ask why

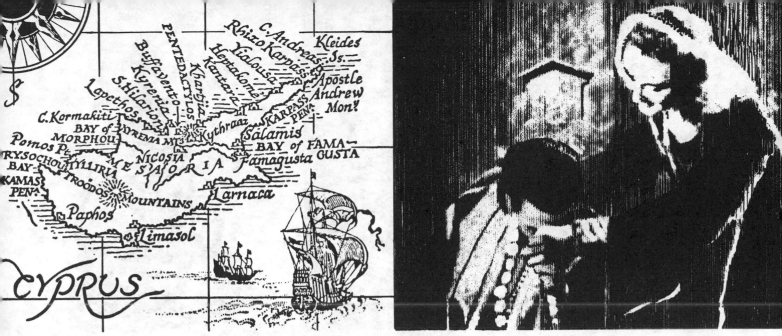

Othello is heartsore because of mistrust

it is possible that there should be such a rapid change in the character of the noble Moor, whose love for Desdemona was boundless. Some critics have argued that the entire action is faulty. Samuel Johnson (1765) believed that Shakespeare did not hesitate to "sacrifice virtue to convenience." And in the present century Mr. E. E. Stoll became convinced that the playwright relied upon a plot convention by means of which the "calumniator" is promptly believed — a mere theatrical convenience. The implication is that the question of probability did not bother the dramatist in the least. But, as the summaries should well establish, Shakespeare did everything possible to render the action probable; and that everything was enough to satisfy audiences from his day unto our own. It must be remembered that Iago succeeded in deceiving all of the other important characters including his wife throughout the first four acts and well into the fifth. Nor should one ignore the fact that such a drastic change as we find in Othello is not unknown in real life and that idealists as well as others are not infrequently imposed upon by hypocrites.

The fact is that Othello is a man who suffers largely from his own virtues, his "free and open disposition," to use Iago's words, and that absoluteness of temperament which may be a desirable characteristic when he is on the field of battle but which hardly fitted him to cope with an archvillain like the ensign. He was never wrong so long as he followed his own instincts; but he was opposed by the most ingenious villain in literature. Simply drawn perhaps Othello is, but he is not drawn as a simpleton.

Iago: Few of the poet's creations have been subject to such wide discussion and divergent points of view as has this villain. For Coleridge, the key to his character was "motiveless malignity," an interpretation that has survived to this day. Related to this view is that which classifies Iago as a Machiavel of the type brought to the stage by Thomas Kyd, Christopher Marlowe, and Shakespeare himself, notably in *Richard III.* Many of the characteristics of this type are to be found in Iago: his dedication to revenge, his utter heartlessness, his mastery of dissembling, his extreme egotism, and his sardonic wit. But he is much more complex in character than the stage Machiavel, as witness his constant improvisations as the action progresses. And if he is a "demi-devil," as he is called in the play, he is a self-made one.

Shakespeare provides the primary motive for Iago's villainy in the first scene of the play: injured vanity. The playwright establishes a second motive, that of sexual jealousy, a bit later. Each of these must be explored carefully as one reads text and summaries. It must suffice here to say that from the first we meet a man of misguided intelligence, one whose mind has been poisoned. He is a victim of excessive pride, or self-love, the first of the Seven Deadly Sins. Literate members of Shakespeare's audience would have recognized this from the very start, familiar as they were with the theological and moral literature of the day. The student's attention is especially invited to the summary comment on Iago's "Virtue? a fig!" speech (I.iii.), which provides a concise explanation of the villain's philosophy of life. Finally, it may be said that Iago is the most intellectual person in the drama, although his is, of course, a completely misguided intellectuality. He fascinates one as, oddly enough, only great evil can somehow hold one's steady interest. It is another tribute to Shakespeare's genius that the playwright never lets us forget that Iago is a human being, not an abstraction.

Desdemona: Here is the refined, socially well-trained daughter of the Venetian senator Brabantio. She has been described as "essentially a passive

13

Capturing Iago after he killed his wife

heroine created to love and suffer," one whose purity and innocence prove her undoing. And she has been referred to as "a sort of child wife, a second Ophelia." But if at times she does manifest a kind of immaturity, as when she chooses the worst possible time to ask her husband to see Cassio and to reconsider the sentence imposed upon him, she remains a spirited young lady who defies convention by eloping with Othello, for whom she shows a rational love, not one based on appetite. To Othello she is no "child wife"; she is his "fair warrior." She can stand firm before him for the sake of what she is convinced is right. It is true that she tells a white lie about the handkerchief (III.iv.86), but if ever there was a pure, unselfish deceiver it is Desdemona. In her innocence she can hardly believe that there are wives who deceive their husbands, and that "some eternal villain" is responsible for her

an introduction to the tragedy of Othello

misery. It is in bewilderment and grief that she meets her terrible fate. She dies heroically, making an effort to protect the husband who had strangled her.

Cassio: We do not see Cassio and Othello together often, yet he remains a pivotal figure. His courtly behavior (II.i. in particular) first provides Iago with the means for starting the chain of events leading to the catastrophe. The lieutenant is absolutely dedicated to the Moor, whose character and martial ability he hardly can praise enough. It was he who spoke most favorably of Othello during the early stages of the courtship, as Desdemona testified. Iago contemptuously refers to him as a Florentine who is no more than what we would call a "desk soldier." But there is conclusive evidence in the play that he won a right to his new appointment in the field of battle as well as in command headquarters. Even the villain concedes that there is a "daily beauty in his life." But Cassio has a fatal defect of which he is aware but upon which Iago capitalizes. Thus like Othello, if at a far different level, he comes for a time to be passion's slave: he temporarily loses his power of reason and he suffers the consequence. If his affair with Bianca offends those of delicate sensibilities, it is to be noted that Shakespeare is careful not to in-

dicate any great irregularity in the relationship of the two. Bianca insists that she is a respectable woman; and, one recalls, she genuinely loved Cassio and wanted to marry him.

Roderigo: This ridiculous dupe, one of the "curled darlings of Venice," who has been *persona non grata* at the household of Brabantio, provides some of the limited comedy in the play. Only the very sentimental will be moved by his pursuit of Desdemona which he himself recognizes as dishonorable. Iago easily capitalizes upon the weakness of Roderigo to his own profit, and it is the villain's remarks in soliloquy which especially reveal what a ridiculous figure the young Venetian is. Admittedly, late in the play, he does show some spirit of a petulant kind: he finally faces up to Iago and threatens to reveal all the details of the plot against the Moor and Cassio. But again he is tenderly led by the nose and is even persuaded to try to kill Cassio. He fails, of course, in this as in all other things, managing only to lose his own life. But Roderigo performs a useful function in the play. His exchanges with Iago give the reader much needed exposition which could be provided otherwise only in soliloquies. Moreover, it is especially he who, in his talks with the villain, provides the means

14

Othello murdering his wife Desdemona

of revealing Iago's basic vulgarity and warped intelligence.

Emilia: Iago's wife is something of an enigma. There is no real evidence of love between her and her husband; indeed, in view of Iago's cynical or downright harsh words to her, one may question whether romance ever entered into their relationship. It has been argued that, among all Shakespeare's characters, she bears closest resemblance to the Nurse in *Romeo and Juliet.* But this can be true only with reference to her earthiness. She does possess a knowledge of the way of the world: witness her talk with Desdemona on the subject of infidelity (IV. iii.58 ff.). If she made a mistake in taking the handkerchief, she did so only in the belief that she was indulging a whim of Iago, and she protests vigorously when he snatches it from her. More serious is her apparent obtuseness at a crucial stage of the action — her failure to see the connection between Othello's strange behavior and the handkerchief. She reaches a stage of complete understanding only after it is too late. But Emelia still invites our sympathy and affection. Most touching is her abiding faith in Desdemona and her courageous defiance of her husband, whom she does not hesitate to denounce as an archvillain — and this at the cost of her own life. Finally she acts as a kind of chorus, often voicing the thoughts that are in our minds. And in her basic goodness she provides a foil to Iago; in her worldliness, to the innocent Desdemona; in her deep faith in the young bride, to Othello.

Brabantio: Curiously the aggrieved father of Dedemona has, on occasion, been looked upon as a rather comical figure: the overly-possessive father who will never allow his daughter to live her own life and thus becomes frantic when he learns that she has eloped with the man of her choice. Such a point of view is to make a contemporary out of Shakespeare and to forget that he was writing during the Renaissance. Desdemona *did* make a "gross revolt" in marrying Othello without her father's permission; she violated a fundamental principle of order and long-established custom. Particularly as the daughter of an aristocratic senator she was subject to her father's guidance in matters relating to betrothal and marriage as in all others. Thus Brabantio was a wronged man, and one can understand that, when he learns that his "jewel" has eloped with a foreigner in the night, however distinguished that foreigner may be, he would bring drastic charges against the Moor.

15

Dramatis Personae

OTHELLO, Moor of Venice.

BRABANTIO, a senator, father to Desdemona.

CASSIO, an honorable lieutenant.

IAGO, an ensign, a villain.

RODERIGO, a gulled gentleman.

DUKE OF VENICE.

SENATORS OF VENICE.

MONTANO, Governor of Cyprus.

GRATIANO, brother to Brabantio.

LODOVICO, kinsman to Brabantio.

CLOWN, servant to Othello.

SAILORS.

DESDEMONA, wife of Othello and daughter of Brabantio.

EMILIA, wife of Iago.

BIANCA, a courtesan, mistress to Cassio.

MESSENGER.

HERALD.

OFFICERS.

VENETIAN GENTLEMEN.

MUSICIANS.

ATTENDANTS.

SCENE—*Venice and Cyprus*

Long since, Samuel Johnson pointed out that *Othello* comes nearer than any of the other great Shakespearean plays, except *The Tempest*, to observing the unities of time, place, and action which were insisted upon by the classical theorists of the Renaissance. Structurally Act I may be regarded as being as a kind of prologue to the play proper. Scenes i and ii might very well have been represented by one scene, and only forty-six lines in scene iii are needed to bring the entire group before the Council Chamber.

As had been Shakespeare's custom since the composition of *Henry V* (1599), we do not meet the tragic hero immediately; indeed we do not even learn his name. What Shakespeare does in this first scene is to set forth the basic elements of the conflict. Othello is referred to as the Moor or by a term which indicates the deep enmity of the speaker. Thus Roderigo calls him "thick lips," the first indication of his dark complexion; and Iago speaks of him as "an old black ram" (88) and as "a Barbary horse" (111), the animal imagery here first introducing the theme of sexuality and of violent revolt against nature in the play.

Iago states his motive for attacking his superior concisely in lines 8-30. At this point one can understand why he has had his defenders: he represents himself as the superior professional soldier who has had to step aside for one Michael Cassio, a man upon whose abilities as a professional soldier he heaps contempt (19-33). Florentines, it may be noted, were known chiefly as financiers and bookkeepers. This would seem to be no more than the proper self-respect of a man who knows his worth, one who through sheer ability has risen in the ranks to a point where the near-highest position is within his reach, and who finds himself relegated to the position of "his Moorship's ancient" (33). But notice his reply when Roderigo asks, in effect, why he should then "follow" the general. He reveals himself as the super-egotist, self-seeking, malicious individual who will use every device in order to advance himself. One should especially note the frequent coarseness of his language (44-48, for example), so revealing of his warped character.

ACT ONE, *scene one.*

(A STREET IN VENICE. NIGHT)

Enter RODERIGO *and* IAGO.

Roderigo. Tush, never tell me! I take it much unkindly
That thou, Iago, who hast had my purse
As if the strings were thine, should'st know of this.
   Iago. 'Sblood, but you will not hear me!   4
If ever I did dream of such a matter,
Abhor me.
   Roderigo. Thou told'st me thou didst hold him in thy hate.
   Iago. Despise me if I do not. Three great ones of the city,
In personal suit to make me his lieutenant,
Off-capped to him; and, by the faith of man,   10
I know my price; I am worth no worse a place.
But he, as loving his own pride and purposes,
Evades them with a bombast circumstance.   13
Horribly stuffed with epithets of war;
And, in conclusion,
Nonsuits my mediators; for, 'Certes,' says he,   16
'I have already chose my officer.'
And what was he?
Forsooth, a great arithmetician,   19
One Michael Cassio, a Florentine
(A fellow almost damned in a fair wife)   21
That never set a squadron in the field,
Nor the division of a battle knows
More than a spinster; unless the bookish theoric,   24
Wherein the toged consuls can propose
As masterly as he. Mere prattle without practice
Is all his soldiership. But he, sir, had th' election;
And I (of whom his eyes had seen the proof
At Rhodes, at Cyprus, and on other grounds
Christian and heathen) must be belee'd and calmed   30
By debitor and creditor; this counter-caster,   31
He, in good time, must his lieutenant be,
And I—God bless the mark!—his Moorship's ancient.   33
   Roderigo. By heaven, I rather would have been his hangman.
   Iago. Why, there's no remedy; 'tis the curse of service.
Preferment goes by letter and affection,
And not by old gradation, where each second   37
Stood heir to th' first. Now, sir, be judge yourself,
Whether I in any just term am affined   39
To love the Moor.
   Roderigo.   I would not follow him then.
   Iago. O, sir, content you;
I follow him to serve my turn upon him.
We cannot all be masters, nor all masters

---

4. " 'Sblood": By God's blood.

10. "Off-capped": Stood with cap in hand.

13. "a bombast circumstance": affected and inflated language.

16. "nonsuits": ignores or rejects. "Certes": Assuredly.

19. "arithmetician": theoretician.

21. "damned in a fair wife": There is obscurity here, for Cassio is not married. Wife may read wise.

24. "bookish theoric": the student, not practitioner.

30. "belee'd and calmed": relegated to a negligible position.

31. "counter-caster": accountant.

33. "ancient": aide-de-camp.

37. "old gradation": traditional order of society.

39. "affined": bound.

17

OTHELLO

Exactly how long he has been capitalizing upon the gullibility of the Venetian dandy, we do not know. The point is that Roderigo emerges as a weak, contemptible figure who is easily victimized.

Iago has just one fixed idea in mind: to avenge himself upon the Moor. And he makes his first move when he induces Roderigo to join him at this late hour of the night in arousing Brabantio and denouncing the general. When the senator appears at a window above, it is first Iago who is the voluble one, informing Brabantio of the elopement and reviling the Moor in the most offensive language. The animal imagery, already referred to, colors his speech. To Shakespeare's audience it would imply that, according to the villain, both the Moor and his bride had been guilty of violating the law of nature, and that the young lady in particular had made what Roderigo calls "a gross revolt" (134) against reason and convention.

Cannot be truly followed. You shall mark
Many a duteous and knee-crooking knave
That, doting on his own obsequious bondage,
Wears out his time, much like his master's ass,
For naught but provender; and when he's old, cashiered. 48
Whip me such honest knaves! Others there are
Who, trimmed in forms and visages of duty, 50
Keep yet their hearts attending on themselves;
And, throwing but shows of service on their lords,
Do well thrive by them, and when they have lined their coats,
Do themselves homage. These fellows have some soul;
And such a one do I profess myself. For, sir,
It is as sure as you are Roderigo,
Were I the Moor, I would not be Iago.
In following him, I follow but myself;
Heaven is my judge, not I for love and duty,
But seeming so, for my peculiar end; 60
For when my outward action doth demonstrate
The native act and figure of my heart 62
In compliment extern, 'tis not long after 63
But I will wear my heart upon my sleeve
For daws to peck at; I am not what I am. 65
Roderigo. What a full fortune does the thick-lips owe 66
If he can carry't thus!
Iago.   Call up her father, 67
Rouse him. Make after him, poison his delight,
Proclaim him in the streets. Incense her kinsmen,
And though he in a fertile climate dwell,
Plague him with flies; though that his joy be joy,
Yet throw such changes of vexation on't
As it may lose some color.
Roderigo. Here is her father's house. I'll call aloud.
Iago. Do, with like timorous accent and dire yell 75
As when, by night and negligence, the fire
Is spied in populous cities.
Roderigo. What, ho, Brabantio! Signior Brabantio, ho!
Iago. Awake! What, ho, Brabantio! Thieves! thieves! thieves!
Look to your house, your daughter, and your bags!
Thieves! thieves!

BRABANTIO *at a window.*

Brabantio. [*above*] What is the reason of this terrible summons?
What is the matter there?
Roderigo. Signior, is all your family within?
Iago. Are your doors locked?
Barbantio.   Why, wherefore ask you this?
Iago. Zounds, sir, y'are robbed! For shame, put on your gown! 86
Your heart is burst; you have lost half your soul.
Even now, now, very now, an old black ram
Is tupping your white ewe. Arise, arise!
Awake the snorting citizens with the bell, 90
Or else the devil will make a grandsire of you.

48. "cashiered": dismissed (but not necessarily without honor).

50. "trimmed": dressed up. "visages": semblances.

60. "peculiar": private.

62. "The native . . . heart": My real thoughts and intent.
63. "compliment extern": outward appearance.
65. "daws": jackdaws, or fools.

66. "thick-lips": the Moor. "owe": own.

67. "carry 't thus": bring off this marriage.

75. "timorous": frightening.

86. "Zounds": by God's wounds.

90. "snorting": snoring.

Arise, I say!

Barbantio. What, have you lost your wits?

Roderigo. Most reverend signior, do you know my
voice?

Brabantio. Not I. What are you?

Roderigo. My name is Roderigo.

Brabantio. The worser welcome!
I have charged thee not to haunt about my doors.
In honest plainness thou hast heard me say
My daughter is not for thee; and now, in madness,
Being full of supper and distemp'ring draughts,   99
Upon malicious bravery dost thou come   100
To start my quiet.   101

Roderigo. Sir, sir, sir —

Brabantio. But thou must needs be sure
My spirit and my place have in them power
To make this bitter to thee.

Roderigo. Patience, good sir.

Brabantio. What tell'st thou me of robbing? This is
Venice;
My house is not a grange.

Roderigo. Most grave Brabantio,   106
In simple and pure soul I come to you.

Iago. Zounds, sir, you are one of those that will not
serve God if the devil bid you. Because we come to
do you service, and you think we are ruffians, you'll
have your daughter covered by a Barbary horse;
you'll have your nephews neigh to you; you'll have   112
coursers for cousins, and gennets for germans.   113

Brabantio. What profane wretch art thou?

Iago. I am one, sir, that comes to tell you your
daughter and the Moor are now making the beast
with two backs.

Brabantio. Thou art a villain.

Iago. You are—a senator.

Brabantio. This thou shalt answer. I know thee,
Roderigo.

Roderigo. Sir, I will answer anything. But I be-
seech you,
If't be your pleasure and most wise consent,
As partly I find it is, that your fair daughter,
At this odd-even and dull watch o' th' night,   123
Transported, with no worse nor better guard
But with a knave of common hire, a gondolier,
To the gross clasps of a lascivious Moor —
If this be known to you, and your allowance,   127
We then have done you bold and saucy wrongs;
But if you know not this, my manners tell me
We have your wrong rebuke. Do not believe
That, from the sense of all civility,   131
I thus would play and trifle with your reverence.
Your daughter, if you have not given her leave,
I say again, hath made a gross revolt,
Tying her duty, beauty, wit, and fortunes
In an extravagant and wheeling stranger   136
Of here and everywhere. Straight satisfy yourself.
If she be in her chamber, or your house,
Let loose on me the justice of the state
For thus deluding you.

99. "distemp'ring draughts": intoxicating drinks.
100. "bravery": defiance, bravado.
101. "start": startle.

106. "grange": isolated farmhouse.

112. "nephews": i.e., grandsons.
113. "gennets for germans": Spanish for relatives.

123. "odd-even": between night and day. "dull": dead.

127. "allowance": approval.

131. "from the sense": in violation.

136. "extravagant and wheeling": vagabond and roving.

As Brabantio moves into action, calling for lights and arousing members of his household, Iago steals away, but not before explaining his reasons for doing so. In his speech (144-159) one learns much of significance about the Moor, who now begins to emerge as a superior public figure, one upon whom the Venetian state depends for its safety. His status as one worthy of being a tragic hero is thus early established. The intensity of Iago's hatred is re-emphasized when the villain states that he hates the general "as he does hell-pains" (154). The diabolic element in his character is here tacitly indicated.

The subsequent action, in which the distraught and almost incredulous father appears frantically questioning Roderigo, concludes the scene in an exciting manner, as Brabantio directs that an armed group led by himself seek out the Moor.

Brabantio.   Strike on the tinder, ho!
Give me a taper! Call up all my people!
This accident is not unlike my dream.   142
Belief of it oppresses me already.
Light, I say! light!   [*Exit above.*

Iago.   Farewell, for I must leave you.
It seems not meet, nor wholesome to my place,
To be produced — as, if I stay, I shall —
Against the Moor. For I do know the state,
However this may gall him with some check,   148
Cannot with safety cast him; for he's embarked   149
With such loud reason to the Cyprus wars,
Which even now stand in act, that for their souls   151
Another of his fathom they have none   152
To lead their business; in which regard,
Though I do hate him as I do hell-pains,
Yet, for necessity of present life,
I must show out a flag and sign of love,
Which is indeed but sign. That you shall surely find
     him,
Lead to the Sagittary the raised search;   158
And there will I be with him. So farewell.   [*Exit.*

Enter, below, BRABANTIO *in his nightgown, and*
          Servants *with torches.*   S.D.

Brabantio. It is too true an evil. Gone she is;
And what's to come of my despised time
Is naught but bitterness. Now Roderigo,
Where didst thou see her? — O unhappy girl! —
With the Moor, say'st thou? — Who would be a
     father? —
How didst thou know 'twas she? — O, she deceives
     me
Past thought! — What said she to you? — Get moe   166
     tapers!
Raise all my kindred! — Are they married, think
     you?
Roderigo. Truly I think they are.
Brabantio. O heaven! How got she out? O treason
     of the blood!
Fathers, from hence trust not your daughters' minds
But what you see them act. Is there not charms
By which the property of youth and maidhood   172
May be abused? Have you not read, Roderigo,
Of some such thing?
Roderigo.   Yes, sir, I have indeed.
Brabantio. Call up my brother. — O, would you
     had had her! —
Some one way, some another. — Do you know
Where we may apprehend her and the Moor?
Roderigo. I think I can discover him, if you please
To get good guard and go along with me.
Brabantio. Pray you lead on. At every house I'll
     call:
I may command at most. — Get weapons, ho!
And raise some special officers of night. —
On, good Roderigo; I'll deserve your pains.   183
          [*Exeunt.*

142. "accident": occurrence.

148. "check": rebuke.
149. "cast": discharge.

151. "stand in act": are going in.
152. "fathom": capacity.

158. "Sagittary": an inn.

S.D. "nightgown": dressing gown.

166. "moe": more.

172. "property": nature.

GONDOLA. (*From a picture of Carpaccio.* 1400.)

183. "deserve": reward.

Scene two.

(ANOTHER STREET)

Enter OTHELLO, IAGO, *and* Attendants *with torches.*

Immediately we find Iago enhancing his public reputation as a trustworthy, honest soldier (1-5). He has been telling Othello that he had inadvertently witnessed the rousing of Brabantio and would have slain Roderigo had he not lacked "iniquity" — a nice ironical touch in view of what we have already learned about him. Othello then speaks just five words (6), and we have the first indication of the character of a man who is in complete control of himself. Especially the student should notice lines 17-28 and 30-32; the Moor is indeed a public officer of great importance; he is no commoner. On the contrary he is of royal descent among the Moors who earlier in history had fought their way to the conquest of Spain and made a valiant effort to conquer all Western Europe.

Othello identifies his bride by name — Desdemona — and speaks with simple but intense feeling of his deep love for her. Not to be ignored is the figure of speech in line 28: "For the sea's worth." If one follows the text carefully he will find the Moor frequently making references to the larger elements in nature, just as he does to the heavens. This is one way in which Shakespeare succeeds in elevating his character to that of the tragic hero.

Consistently, he rejects Iago's advice to retire (30): he is not one to seek to avoid facing Brabantio and the armed group. It is not mere boasting by any means when he says: "My parts, my title, and my perfect soul/Shall manifest me rightly" (31-32). Here is the noble Moor, commanding respect and admiration.

Iago. Though in the trade of war I have slain men,
Yet do I hold it very stuff o' th' conscience
To do no contrived murther. I lack iniquity
Sometimes to do me service. Nine or ten times
I had thought t' have yerked him here under the
    ribs.   5
Othello. 'Tis better as it is.
Iago.   Nay, but he prated,
And spoke such scurvy and provoking terms
Against your honor
That with the little godliness I have
I did full hard forbear him. But I pray you, sir,
Are you fast married? Be assured of this,   11
That the magnifico is much beloved,   12
And hath in his effect a voice potential   13
As double as the Duke's. He will divorce you,   14
Or put upon you what restraint and grievance
The law, with all his might to enforce it on,
Will give him cable.
Othello.   Let him do his spite.   17
My services which I have done the signiory   18
Shall out-tongue his complaints. 'Tis yet to know —   19
Which, when I know that boasting is an honor,
I shall promulgate — I fetch my life and being
From men of royal siege; and my demerits   22
May speak unbonneted to as proud a fortune   23
As this that I have reached. For know, Iago,   24
But that I love the gentle Desdemona,
I would not my unhoused free condition   26
Put into circumscription and confine
For the sea's worth.

Enter CASSIO, *with torches,* Officers.

                But look, what lights come yond?
Iago. Those are the raised father and his friends.
You were best go in.
Othello.   Not I; I must be found.
My parts, my title, and my perfect soul   31
Shall manifest me rightly. It is they?
Iago. By Janus, I think no.   33
Othello. The servants of the Duke, and my lieu-
    tenant.
The goodness of the night upon you, friends!
What is the news?
Cassio.   The Duke does greet you general;
And he requires your haste-post-haste appearance
Even on the instant.

5. "yerked": stabbed.

11. "fast": securely.

12. "magnifico": grandee (i.e., Brabantio).
13. "potential": powerful.
14. "double": doubly influential.

17. "cable": rope.
18. "signiory": Venetian government.
19. "yet to know": not yet generally known.

22. "siege": rank.
    "demerits": deserts.
23-24. "May . . . reached": Without boasting I may say that my merits match those of my wife's family.

26. "unhoused": unrestrained.

31. "parts": abilities.
    "perfect soul": stainless conscience.

33. "Janus": two faced god of the Romans.

OTHELLO

ACT I SCENE II

Cassio, whom we now see and hear for the first time, has arrived with the Duke's message of great import relating to the Turkish threat to the island of Cyprus, key to the defense of Venice. Once more Othello's high status is indicated. In this late hour of the night the Duke and the assembled council have "hotly called" for him. Before Iago can take advantage of the Moor's brief absence from the stage and tell Cassio of the elopement, the general is ready to leave for the Council Chamber.

It is at this point that Brabantio and his party confront Othello, denouncing him as a thief. Both sides draw their weapons, Iago effectively continuing his pose of the soldier loyal to his commander as he challenges Roderigo (58). The Moor's brief speech which follows speaks volumes as regards his stability and generalship. He is the very soul of self-possession, commanding both sides to sheathe their swords and courteously addressing Brabantio, who, he says, needs no weapons to command him.

And now the grief-stricken father has his first chance to denounce his unwanted son-in-law. So incredulous have been the facts of the elopement been to him that he is sure the Moor has used some sort of charms or drugs to win his daughter. The marriage seems to him to be monstrous in the sense that it represents a deviation from that which is natural. How else, he asks, in effect, would Desdemona, carefully reared as she has been, have so brought scandal upon herself and her father by running to the Moor's "sooty bosom" (70)?

Othello.   What's the matter, think you?
Cassio. Something from Cyprus, as I may divine.
It is a business of some heat. The galleys   40
Have sent a dozen sequent messengers   41
This very night at one another's heels,
And many of the consuls, raised and met,
Are at the Duke's already. You have been hotly
　　called for;
When, being not at your lodging to be found,
The Senate hath sent about three several quests
To search you out.
Othello.   'Tis well I am found by you.
I will but spend a word here in the house,
And go with you.   [*Exit.*
Cassio.   Ancient, what makes he here?
Iago. Faith, he to-night hath boarded a land carack   50
If it prove lawful prize, he's made for ever.
Cassio. I do not understand.
Iago.   He's married.
Cassio.   To who?

Enter OTHELLO.

Iago. Marry, to — Come, captain, will you go?
Othello.   Have with you.
Cassio. Here comes another troop to seek for you.

Enter BRABANTIO, RODERIGO, *and others with lights
　　and weapons.*

Iago. It is Brabantio. General, be advised.
He comes to bad intent.
Othello.   Holla! stand there!
Roderigo. Signior, it is the Moor.
Brabantio.   Down with him, thief!
　　[*They draw on both sides.*
Iago. You, Roderigo! Come, sir, I am for you.
Othello. Keep up your bright swords, for the dew
　　will rust them.   59
Good signior, you shall more command with years
Than with your weapons.
Brabantio. O thou foul thief, where has thou stowed
　　my daughter?
Damned as thou art, thou hast enchanted her!
For I'll refer me to all things of sense,
If she in chains of magic were not bound,
Whether a maid so tender, fair, and happy,
So opposite to marriage that she shunned
The wealthy curled darlings of our nation,
Would ever have, t' incur a general mock,
Run from her guardage to the sooty bosom
Of such a thing as thou — to fear, not to delight.
Judge me the world if 'tis not gross in sense   72
That thou hast practiced on her with foul charms,
Abused her delicate youth with drugs or minerals
That weaken motion. I'll have't disputed on;   75
'Tis probable, and palpable to thinking.
I therefore apprehend and do attach thee   77

GENERAL OF VENICE, IN TIME OF WAR.

40. "galleys": officers of the galleys.

41. "sequent": consecutive.

50. "carack": large trading ship.

59. "Keep up": sheathe.

72. "gross in sense": perfectly clear.

75. "motion": sense.
"disputed on": legally argued.

77. "attach": arrest.

For an abuser of the world, a practicer
Of arts inhibited and out of warrant.   79
Lay hold upon him. If he do resist,
Subdue him at his peril.
   Othello.   Hold your hands,
Both you of my inclining and the rest.   82
Were it my cue to fight, I should have known it
Without a prompter. Where will you that I go
To answer this your charge?
   Brabantio.   To prison, till fit time
Of law and course of direct session   86
Call thee to answer.
   Othello.   What if I do obey?
How may the Duke therewith satisfied,
Whose messengers are here about my side
Upon some present business of the state   90
To bring me to him?
   Officer.   'Tis true, most worthy signior.
The Duke's in council, and your noble self
I am sure is sent for.
   Brabantio.   How? The Duke in council?
In this time of the night? Bring him away.
Mine's not an idle cause. The Duke himself,   95
Or any of my brothers of the state,
Cannot but feel this wrong as 'twere their own;
For if such actions may have passage free,   98
Bondslaves and pagans shall our statesmen be.
                      [*Exeunt*.

79. "inhibited": prohibited.
    "out of warrant": unjustifiable.

82. "inclining": party.

86. "course of direct session": due course of law.

90. "present": immediate.

95. "idle": trivial.

98. "have . . . free": be freely allowed

> Again Othello displays himself as the admirably self-possessed master of the situation. When armed conflict once more threatens, he controls matters easily. (See especially lines 81-85). He is willing to answer all charges brought against him. In view of the Duke's summons, Brabantio, despite his prerogatives as a Venetian aristocrat and senator, finds that he cannot force the imprisonment of the Moor. But the aggrieved father consoles himself: the Duke himself and the other senators will surely "feel this wrong as 'twere their own" (97).

Scene three.

(A COUNCIL CHAMBER)

Enter DUKE *and* Senators, *sitting at a table, with lights and* Attendants.

Duke. There is no composition in these news   1
That gives them credit.
   1. Senator.   Indeed they are disproportioned.
My letters say a hundred and seven galleys.
   Duke. And mine a hundred forty.
   2. Senator.   And mine two hundred.
But though they jump not on a just account —   5
As in these cases where the aim reports   6
'Tis oft with difference — yet do they all confirm
A Turkish fleet, and bearing up to Cyprus.   8
   Duke. Nay, it is possible enough to judgment.
I do not so secure me in the error   10
But the main article I do approve   11
In fearful sense.
   Sailor. [*within*] What, ho! what, ho! what ho!   12
   Officer. A messenger from the galleys.

Enter Sailor.

   Duke.   Now, what's the business?
   Sailor. The Turkish preparation makes for Rhodes.

1. "composition": consistency.

5. "jump": agree.
6. "aim reports": make conjectures about reports, which do not often agree in detail.
8. "bearing up": making course for.

10. "so secure me": take such comfort.
11. "article": substance.
    "approve": accept.
12. "fearful": to be feared.

> Assembled in the Venetian Council Chamber are the governing body of the state, headed by the Duke. All are pondering the news which has been sent to them from Cyprus and from which they find no clear statement as to the size of the Turkish fleet nor its exact destination. None, however, underestimates the danger involved: each is sure that the enemy intends to move against the Venetians by attacking Cyprus, despite the fact that a newly arrived sailor reports that one Signior Angelo, who is not identified here nor heard of again, insists that the Turks "make for Rhodes." The first senator argues that, in view of the importance of Cyprus, an island which the enemy covets, the apparent move toward Rhodes is an obvious ruse to catch the Cyprians off guard. The Duke agrees. Then a messenger from Montano, Governor of the island, confirms the Council's conclusion: it is Cyprus which the enemy intends to attack.

OTHELLO

ACT I SCENE III

At this point of the action Brabantio, Othello, Iago, Roderigo, and officers enter the Chamber. The fact that the Duke addresses Othello, not even seeing Brabantio at first (48-50), is another indication of the extent to which Venice places its hopes on the "valiant" Moor — more evidence, that is, of his high status as the hero of the play.

So was I bid report here to the state
By Signior Angelo.

Duke. How say you by this change?
1. Senator.   This cannot be
By no assay of reason. 'Tis a pageant   18
To keep us in false gaze. When we consider   19
Th' importancy of Cyprus to the Turk,
And let ourselves again but understand
That, as it more concerns the Turk than Rhodes,
So may he with more facile question bear it,   23
For that it stands not in such warlike brace,   24
But altogether lacks th' abilities
That Rhodes is dressed in — if we make thought of this,
We must not think the Turk is so unskillful
To leave that latest which concerns him first,
Neglecting an attempt of ease and gain
To wake and wage a danger profitless.   30
  Duke. Nay, in all confidence he's not for Rhodes.
  Officer. Here is more news.

Enter a Messenger.

  Messenger. The Ottomites, reverend and gracious,   33
Steering with due course toward the isle of Rhodes,
Have there injointed them with an after fleet.   35
  1. Senator. Ay, so I thought. How many, as you guess?
  Messenger. Of thirty sail; and now they do restem   37
Their backward course, bearing with frank appearance   38
Their purposes toward Cyprus. Signior Montano,
Your trusty and most valiant servitor,
With his free duty recommends you thus,   41
And prays you to believe him.
  Duke. 'Tis certain then for Cyprus.
Marcus Luccicos, is not he in town?
  1. Senator. He's now in Florence.
  Duke. Write from us to him; post, post-haste dispatch.

Enter BRABANTIO, OTHELLO, CASSIO, IAGO, RODERIGO,
and Officers.

  1. Senator. Here comes Brabantio and the valiant Moor.
  Duke. Valiant Othello, we must straight employ you
Against the general enemy Ottoman.
[*To Brabantio*] I did not see you. Welcome, gentle signior.
We lacked your counsel and your help to-night.
  Brabantio. So did I yours. Good your grace, pardon me.
Neither my place, nor aught I heard of business,
Hath raised me from my bed; nor doth the general care
Take hold on me; for my particular grief   55
Is of so floodgate and o'erbearing nature   56

18. "assay": test.
    "pageant": show.
19. "in false gaze": looking the wrong way.

23. "with . . . bear": more easily made captive.
24. "brace": stance of defense.

30. "wake and wage": rouse and risk.

33. "Ottomites": Turks.

35. "injointed": joined.

37. "restem": steer again.

38. "frank appearance": no attempt to conceal.

41. "With . . . thus": With proper respect thus advises.

55. "particular": personal.
56. "floodgate": torrential.

OTHELLO

ACT I SCENE III

Matters of state are not immediately discussed further. Brabantio, because of his prerogatives as a senator and an aristocrat, has the opportunity to make his startling charge and to appeal for help. So violent is the expression of his grief that at first the Duke and the others believe that Desdemona must be dead. Then they are told that she had been "stol'n" from her father by one who made use of "spells and medicines bought of mountebanks" (61). How else to explain how the law of nature could have been so violated? The Duke promptly assures Brabantio that the culprit, be he even the Duke's son, will be dealt with in accordance with the "bloody book of the law" (67). It is then that the aggrieved father points to Othello as the man against whom these charges are brought. There is much meaning packed into the response of all members of the Council: "we are sorry for't" (73). That the general of their choice should be so accused is a matter of great consternation.

Now we come to the first of Othello's great speeches, for he belongs to that select group of superior speakers and poets among Shakespeare's heroes (76 ff.). There is much to be noted and remembered in this speech, for it will help us to understand why such a noble, stable individual would come to reject reason and become passion's slave. With simple dignity the Moor addresses the group, conceding that he has married Brabantio's daughter, but tacitly denying that he was able to do so by means of witchcraft upon which the senator insisted. He presents himself as a man who has spent almost all of his life in the field as an active soldier. The principle of decorum, derived from classical theory, had it that the soldier did not possess nor cherish the arts which belong to peace; he is to be depicted as honest, straight-forward, often rather blunt. Without being a Philistine, he does not indulge in eloquence or nice verbal amenities; he is a man of action. Thus Othello describes himself as "Rude . . . in speech" and "little blessed with the soft arts of peace" (81-2). He admits that he knows little of the world save that which pertains to warfare. Now Iago, present in the Council Chamber will remember these words, as he will those of Brabantio.

The father enlarges upon his earlier charge, arguing that it is impossible that his daughter, "A maiden never bold" (94), should have fallen in love "with what she feared to look on!"—another reference to Othello's race and

That it engluts and swallows other sorrows,	57
And it is still itself.	
Duke. Why, what's the matter?	
Brabantio. My daughter! O, my daughter!	
All. Dead?	
Barbantio. Ay, to me.	
She is abused, stol'n from me, and corrupted	
By spells and medicines bought of mountebanks;	61
For nature so prepost'rously to err,	
Being not deficient, blind, or lame of sense,	63
Sans witchcraft could not.	
Duke. Whoe'er he be that in this foul proceeding	
Hath thus beguiled your daughter of herself,	66
And you of her, the bloody book of law	
You shall yourself read in the bitter letter	
After your own sense; yea, though our proper son	69
Stood in your action.	
Brabantio. Humbly I thank your grace.	70
Here is the man — this Moor, whom now, it seems,	
Your special mandate for the state affairs	
Hath hither brought.	
All. We are very sorry for't.	
Duke [*to Othello*] What, in your own part, can you	
say to this?	
Brabantio. Nothing, but this is so.	
Othello. Most potent, grave, and reverend signiors,	
My very noble, and approved good masters,	77
That I have ta'en away this old man's daughter,	
It is most true; true I have married her.	
The very head and front of my offending	80
Hath this extent, no more. Rude am I in my speech,	81
And little blessed with the soft phrase of peace;	
For since these arms of mine had seven years' pith	83
Till now some nine moons wasted, they have used	
Their dearest action in the tented field;	85
And little of this great world can I speak	
More than pertains to feats of broil and battle;	
And therefore little shall I grace my cause	
In speaking for myself. Yet, by your gracious	
patience,	
I will a round unvarnished tale deliver	90
Of my whole course of love — what drugs, what	
charms,	
What conjuration, and what mighty magic	
(For such proceeding am I charged withal)	
I won his daughter.	
Brabantio. A maiden never bold;	
Of spirit so still and quiet that her motion	95
Blushed at herself; and she — in spite of nature,	96
Of years, of country, credit, everything —	97
To fall in love with what she feared to look on!	
It is a judgment maimed and most imperfect	
That will confess perfection so could err.	100
Against all rules of nature, and must be driven	
To find out practices of cunning hell	102
Why this should be. I therefore vouch again	103
That with some mixtures pow'rful o'er the blood,	104
Or with some dram, conjured to this effect,	105
He wrought upon her.	

57. "engluts": devours.

61. "mountebanks": charlatans who sell quack medicine.

63. "deficient": weak-minded.

66. "beguiled . . . herself": i.e., caused your daughter to be at odds with herself.

69. "our proper": my own.

70. "stood . . . action": were accused by you.

77. "approved": tested.

80. "front": forehead.
81. "Rude": Unpolished.

83. "pith": strength.

85. "dearest": most important.

90. "round": unadorned.

95-96. "her . . . blushed": so shy that she blushed at the slightest cause.
97. "credit": reputation.

100. "will confess": would believe.

102. "practices": plots.

103. "vouch": declare.
104. "blood": passions.
105. "conjured": mixed with spells.

physical appearance in contrast to the native Venetians. He refers to his daughter's behavior as erring "against all nature" (101) and as her having become the victim of hellish practices.

Quite reasonably the Duke points out that Brabantio must substantiate his charges. And when the first senator (the voice of the others) point blank asks the Moor if the charges are true, Othello asks that the lady be brought before the Council to speak for herself, adding that if he is found to be guilty by her testimony, he will not protest any sentence imposed upon him. Iago, with some attendants, is sent to escort her to the Council Chamber. While the group await Desdemona's arrival, Othello gives his explanation of the matter in the second and longer of his memorable speeches. (76)

We learn that Brabantio himself had shown his high regard for the general, often inviting the Moor to his house and urging him to tell the story of his exciting life filled with "disastrous chances," "moving accidents by flood and field," and "hairbreadth scapes" (134-6). Lines 140-145 are the ones which, it is widely held, derive from Philemon Holland's translation of Pliny's *Natural History* (1601) — sometimes referred to as *Unnatural History* in view of the fabulous things described therein. Little wonder that Desdemona would become enthralled by the account given by a man of action who contrasted so much with the "wealthy curled darlings" of Venice, and that she soon came to love Othello. This was the only "witchcraft" that he used, the Moor concludes, as Desdemona enters accompanied by the apparently indispensable Iago and the attendants.

Duke.   To vouch this is no proof,
Without more certain and more overt test
Than these thin habits and poor likelihoods -   108
Of modern seeming do prefer against him.   109
  1. Senator. But, Othello, speak.
Did you by indirect and forced courses   111
Subdue and poison this young maid's affections?
Or came it by request, and such fair question   113
As soul to soul affordeth?
  Othello.   I do beseech you,
Send for the lady to the Sagittary   115
And let her speak of me before her father.
If you do find me foul in her report,
The trust, the office, I do hold of you
Not only take away, but let your sentence
Even fall upon my life.
  Duke.   Fetch Desdemona hither.
  Othello. Ancient, conduct them; you best know
    the place.

[*Exit* IAGO, *with two or three* Attendants.]

And till she come, as truly as to heaven
I do confess the vices of my blood,
So justly to your grave ears I'll present
How I did thrive in this fair lady's love,
And she in mine.
  Duke. Say it, Othello.
  Othello. Her father loved me, oft invited me;
Still questioned me the story of my life   129
From year to year — the battles, sieges, fortunes
That I have passed.
I ran it through, even from my boyish days
To th' very moment that he bade me tell it.
Wherein I spake of most disastrous chances,
Of moving accidents by flood and field;
Of hairbreadth scapes i' th' imminent deadly
    breach;
Of being taken by the insolent foe
And sold to slavery; of my redemption thence
And portance in my travel's history;   139
Wherein of anters vast and deserts idle,   140
Rough quarries, rocks, and hills whose heads touch
    heaven
It was my hint to speak — such was the process;   142
And of the Cannibals that each other eat,
The Anthropophagi, and men whose heads   144
Do grow beneath their shoulders. This to hear
Would Desdemona seriously incline;
But still the house affairs would draw her thence;
Which ever as she could with haste dispatch,
She'd come again, and with a greedy ear
Devour up my discourse. Which I observing,
Took once a pliant hour, and found good means   151
To draw from her a prayer of earnest heart
That I would all my pilgrimage dilate,   153
Whereof by parcels she had something heard,   154
But not intentively. I did consent   155
And often did beguile her of her tears
When I did speak of some distressful stroke

108. "thin habits": slight semblances.
109. "modern seeming": daily supposition.
    "prefer": bring a charge against.
111. "forced": violent.

113. "question": conversation.

115. "Sagittary": an inn designated by a sign depicting Sagittarius, the centaur of the zodiac, the fictional animal compounded of a man and a horse and armed with bow and arrow.

129. "Still": Continually.

139. "portance": behavior.
140. "anters": caves.
    "idle": barren.

142. "hint": occasion, or opportunity.

144. "Anthropophagi": man-eaters.

151. "pliant": convenient.

153. "dilate": tell fully.
154. "parcels": portions.
155. " intentively": with full attention.

OTHELLO

ACT I SCENE III

It is at this point, turning to Brabantio, the Duke expresses his belief that his own daughter would have been won by such a tale, and he urges the senator to reconcile himself to the circumstances. But the latter still insists that Desdemona be heard, still convinced as he is that his view must be the correct one. Indeed he is so sure that he promises, in effect, to withdraw all charges against the Moor if his daughter proves to be "half the wooer" (176-8). In affectionate terms he then addresses Desdemona and asks where, among all present, she most owes obedience. The young lady replies in ten lines: hers is now a "divided duty" (181): she remains bound to her noble father for her "life and education" (182); he remains her "lord of duty" (184), and she will always honor him as such. Now she has a husband; she must recognize her duties to him just as her mother did to her father. Brabantio knows that he is a defeated man, that his ideas of how the Moor had "stolen" his daughter are completely wrong. Here indeed is a man who is crushed, one who will never reconcile himself to the fact that his "jewel" should have renounced paternal guidance and secretly have married a man of a different race and nation.

That my youth suffered. My story being done,
She gave me for my pains a world of sighs.
She swore, i' faith, 'twas strange, 'twas passing
    strange;
'Twas pitiful, 'twas wondrous pitiful.
She wished she had not heard it; yet she wished
That heaven had made her such a man. She thanked
    me;   163
And bade me, if I had a friend that loved her,
I should but teach him how to tell my story,
And that would woo her. Upon this hint I spake.
She loved me for the dangers I had passed,
And I loved her that she did pity them.
This only is the witchcraft I have used.
Here comes the lady. Let her witness it.

Enter DESDEMONA, IAGO, Attendants

Duke. I think this tale would win my daughter too.
Good Brabantio,
Take up this mangled matter at the best.   173
Men do their broken weapons rather use
Than their bare hands.
   Brabantio.   I pray you hear her speak.
If she confess that she was half the wooer,
Destruction on my head if my bad blame
Light on the man! Come thither, gentle mistress.
Do you perceive in all this noble company
Where most you owe obedience?
   Desdemona.   My noble father,
I do perceive here a divided duty.
To you I am bound for life and education;   182
My life and education both do learn me
How to respect you: you are the lord of duty;
I am hitherto your daughter. But here's my
    husband;
And so much duty as my mother showed
To you, preferring you before her father,
So much I challenge that I may profess   188
Due to the Moor my lord.
   Brabantio.   God b' wi' ye! I have done.
Please it your grace, on to the state affairs.
I had rather to adopt a child than get it.   191
Come hither, Moor.
I here do give thee that with all my heart
Which, but thou hast already, with all my heart
I would keep from thee. For your sake, jewel,   195
I am glad at soul I have no other child;
For thy escape would teach me tyranny,   197
To hang clogs on them. I have done, my lord.
   Duke. Let me speak like yourself and lay a sen-
    tence   199
Which, as a grise or step, may help these lovers   200
(Into your favor.)
When remedies are past, the griefs are ended
By seeing the worst, which late on hopes depended.
To mourn a mischief that is past and gone
Is the next way to draw new mischief on.
What cannot be preserved when fortune takes,
Patience her injury a mock'ry makes.

163. "her": for her.

173. "take . . . best": make the best you can of this confused affair.

182. "education": upbringing.

188. "challenge": claim the right.

191. "get": beget.

195. "For your sake": because of you.

197. "escape": escapade.

199. "like yourself": as you should speak. "sentence": maxim.
200. "grise": degree.

OTHELLO

ACT I SCENE III

The Duke endeavors to console the father again by voicing familiar maxims, for in his present role he can be nothing but sententious. The gist of his counsel is that what is done is done, that it does no one any good to "mourn a mischief that is past and gone" (202-9). But the heart-broken Brabantio finds little comfort in these words which, he says, cannot heal the "bruised heart." And so all now turn their attention to official business.

Othello is informed that the Turks plan to attack Cyprus and that he, as the leader best informed about the fortifications of the island, must ignore personal desires and turn his full attention upon the enterprise against the Turks. Thus a new element is introduced. It would seem that the lovers are to be separated immediately. As another indication of his high character, Othello promptly acknowledges that public duty takes precedence over private desires; so he had been schooled in his long career as a soldier. He asks only that his wife be looked after in a manner befitting a lady of her rank. When the Duke suggests that she return to her father's household Brabantio, Othello and Desdemona reject the suggestion at once. Again showing her spirit as in her earlier speech, it is the young bride who speaks out at greatest length (241 ff.). Aware that her presence would only agonize her father, she pleads with the Duke to be allowed to go with her husband and expresses her abiding love for the Moor — a love, be it noted again — based upon her recognition of "his honors and valiant parts." The general joins her in the suit (260 ff.), and we have another speech which invites sympathy and admiration for him: his too is a rational love; he wishes only "to be free and bounteous to her mind."

The robbed that smiles steals something from the thief;
He robs himself that spends a bootless grief.   209
Brabantio. So let the Turk of Cyprus us beguile:
We lose it not so long as we can smile.
He bears the sentence well that nothing bears
But the free comfort which from thence he hears;
But he bears both the sentence and the sorrow
That to pay grief must of poor patience borrow.
These sentences, to sugar, or to gall,
Being strong on both sides, are equivocal.   217
But words are words. I never yet did hear
That the bruised heart was pierced through the ear.
Beseech you, now to the affairs of state.

Duke. The Turk with a most mighty preparation
makes for Cyprus. Othello, the fortitude of the   222
place is best known to you; and though we have
there a substitute of most allowed sufficiency, yet   224
opinion, a sovereign mistress of effects, throws a   225
more safer voice on you. You must therefore be
content to slubber the gloss of your new fortunes   227
with this more stubborn and boisterous expedition.

Othello. The tyrant custom, most grave senators,
Hath made the flinty and steel couch of war
My thrice-driven bed of down. I do agnize   231
A natural and prompt alacrity
I find in hardness; and do undertake
These present wars against the Ottomites.
Most humbly, therefore, bending to your state,
I crave fit disposition for my wife,
Due reference of place, and exhibition,   237
With such accommodation and besort   238
As levels with her breeding.

Duke.   If you please,   239
Be't at her father's.

Brabantio.   I'll not have it so.

Othello. Nor I.

Desdemona.   Nor I. I would not there reside,
To put my father in impatient thoughts
By being in his eye. Most gracious Duke,
To my unfolding lend your prosperous ear,   244
And let me find a charter in your voice,   245
To assist my simpleness.   246

Duke. What would you, Desdemona?

Desdemona. That I did love the Moor to live
    with him,
My downright violence, and storm of fortunes,   249
May trumpet to the world. My heart's subdued
Even to the very quality of my lord.   251
I saw Othello's visage in his mind,
And to his honors and his valiant parts
Did I my soul and fortunes consecrate.
So that, dear lords, if I be left behind,
A moth of peace, and he go to the war,   256
The rites for which I love him are bereft me,
And I a heavy interim shall support
By his dear absence. Let me go with him.

Othello. Let her have your voices.

209. "bootless": vain.

217. "equivocal": equal.

222. "fortitude": fortification.

224. "allowed": acknowledged.
225. "opinion": public opinion.

227. "slubber": sully.

231. "thrice-driven": thoroughly sifted. "agnize": acknowledge.

237. "reference": assignment. "exhibition": provision.
238. "besort": suitable company.

239. "levels with": befits.

244. "unfolding": revealing. "prosperous": propitious.
245. "charter": privilege.
246. "simpleness": lack of skill.

249. "My . . . fortunes": the way in which I have so abruptly acted in this matter.
251. "quality": profession.

256. "A moth of peace": A useless creature living a luxurious life.

OTHELLO

ACT I SCENE III

Above all, he will at no time allow her presence to interfere with his public duty. The modern meaning of defunct (264) is not applicable here. Othello is merely stating, as it were, that he is not one to essay the role of a Troilus or an Antony, whose infatuation did cause them to ignore public obligations.

The Duke tells Othello that he can make what arrangements he likes. The important thing is that he must leave this very night for "Th' affair calls haste." Desdemona is somewhat taken aback by this order. But notice the Moor's reply: "With all my heart" (278). Immediately there remains only for him to leave some trusted officer behind, one who will see to it that the young lady is brought to Cyprus safely. Othello has just the man for this assignment — "honest" Iago. The Duke concurs, says his farewells to the group, and — sententious as ever — again has words of consolation for Brabantio (289-90). But sententious or not, his lines add to the public testimony of Othello's worth, his superiority. More important are the two lines spoken by Brabantio to the Moor just before the senator leaves with other members of the Council (292-3). These, as we shall find, are packed with irony and provide, in part, an example of drastic presaging (that is, a way of anticipating subsequent action in the play.) And so with reference to Othello's reply: "My life upon her faith." Othello then gives brief directions to Iago and escorts Desdemona from The Council Chamber. "We must obey the time," he concludes (300) — further evidence of his dedication to duty.

Iago and Roderigo are left alone on stage. Appropriately, in view of the subject of their discourse, the medium is shifted to prose, for poetry (here specifically blank verse with occasional couplets) idealizes expression.

Roderigo, ironically addressed as "noble heart" by Iago, then presents himself as the tormented, rejected lover who can find relief from his misery only in suicide. Let it be noted that his completely intemperate, irrational love provides a marked contrast to the noble, completely rational love of Othello for Desdemona. Iago scoffs at him, and we get an introduction to the villain's moral philosophy which is expounded in greater detail in his next speech. More revealing is Iago's statement that he has "never found man that knew how to love himself" (313-14). He certainly has established himself already as one who does not "err" in this respect.

Vouch with me, heaven, I therefore beg it not   261
To please the palate of my appetite,
Nor to comply with heat — the young affects   263
In me defunct — and proper satisfaction;
But to be free and bounteous to her mind;   265
And heaven defend your good souls that you think   266
I will your serious and great business scant
For she is with me. No, when light-winged toys   268
Of feathered Cupid seel with wanton dullness   269
My speculative and officed instruments,   270
That my disports corrupt and taint my business,   271
Let housewives make a skillet of my helm,
And all indign and base adversities   273
Make head against my estimation!   274
Duke. Be it as you shall privately determine,
Either for her stay or going. Th' affair cries haste,
And speed must answer it. You must hence to-night.
(*Desdemona.* To-night, my lord?
Duke.   This night.)
Othello.   With all my heart.
Duke. At nine i' th' morning here we'll meet again.
Othello, leave some officer behind,
And he shall our commission bring to you,
With such things else of quality and respect
As doth import you.
Othello.   So please your grace, my ancient;   283
A man he is of honesty and trust.
To his conveyance I assign my wife,
With what else needful your good grace shall think
To be sent after me.
Duke.   Let it be so.
Good night to every one. [*to Brabantio*] And, noble
     signior,
If virtue no delighted beauty lack,   289
Your son-in-law is far more fair than black.
1. Senator. Adieu, brave Moor. Use Desdemona
     well.
Brabantio. Look to her, Moor, if thou hast eyes
     to see:
She has deceived her father, and may thee.

          [*Exit* DUKE, Senators, Officers, *etc.*

Othello. My life upon her faith! — Honest Iago,
My Desdemona must I leave to thee.
I prithee let thy wife attend on her,
And bring them after in the best advantage.   297
Come, Desdemona. I have but an hour
Of love, of worldly matters and direction,
To spend with thee. We must obey the time.
          [*Exit* MOOR, *and* DESDEMONA.
Roderigo. Iago, —
Iago. What say'st thou, noble heart?
Roderigo. What will I do, think'st thou?
Iago. Why, go to bed and sleep.
Roderigo. I will incontinently drown myself.   305
Iago. If thou dost, I shall never love thee after.
Why, thou silly gentleman!
Roderigo. It is silliness to live when to live is torment; and then have we a prescription to die when death is our physician.

261. "Vouch": certify.

263. "heat": passions. "young affects": youthful tendencies.
265. "bounteous": generous.
266. "defend": forbid.

268. "For": because.
269. "seel": blind.
270. "My . . . instruments": my perceptive and responsible faculties.
271. "That": so that.

273. "indign": unworthy.
274. "estimation": reputation.

283. "import": concern.

289. "delighted": delightful.

297. "in . . . advantage": at the best opportunity.

305. "incontinently": straightway.

Thus the key to his character is clearly given to us: excessive, unwarranted pride, or self-love, the first of the Seven Deadly Sins. His attitude toward love between man and woman is also made clear by his reference to "a guinea hen" and a "baboon." Once more all this will be clarified by his longer speech which soon follows. That passion controls Roderigo's will is made especially apparent by the young Venetian's statement: "I confess it is my shame to be so fond (foolish), but it is not my virtue (temperament) to amend it" (317-19). And this gives Iago the proper introduction to a fifteen-line summary of his moral philosophy in a speech which at once reveals his knowledge of contemporary theory and, more important, his perversion of the widely accepted doctrine relating to reason, the will, and concupiscence or appetite. To explain it as briefly and simply as possible, let it be understood that the Renaissance inherited from classical and medieval moral philosophy the belief that reason was, to use the language of Shakespeare's day, "the Queen of the powers of the soul," directing all that these powers should embrace or avoid and never going wrong so long as it contained itself within the bounds and order presented by nature. Reason, as Iago states, makes it possible for men "to cool our raging motions, our carnal stings, our unbitted lusts" (332-33). But, contrary to the orthodox view on the subject, the ensign elevates will, or desire, over both reason and appetite: "Our bodies are our gardens, to which our wills are gardeners . . . why, the power and corrigible authority . . . lies in our wills" (321-27). He thus rejects the conclusion reached, for example, by Aristotle and by St. Thomas Aquinas (to name two especially distinguished moralists) and generally accepted in Shakespeare's day. In his extreme egotism, he is convinced that what he wills need not be subjected to the test of reason; he is sure that he can control his passions. But, ironically, one has only to turn back to Act I, scene i to see him revealed as a man enslaved by the passions of envy and the desire for revenge. Moreover, as has been stated earlier, it is he who first introduces the theme of sexual jealousy and lust in the play.

Iago convinces the pathetically comic Roderigo that his chances are now even better for his gaining the love of Desdemona — if he continues giving more money to Iago. Point by point the ensign gives his reasons: the elopement

Iago. O villainous! I have looked upon the world for four times seven years; and since I could distinguish betwixt a benefit and an injury, I never found man that knew how to love himself. Ere I would say I would drown myself for the love of a guinea hen, I would change my humanity with a baboon.

Roderigo. What should I do? I confess it is my shame to be so fond, but it is not in my virtue to amend it.

Iago. Virtue? a fig! 'Tis in ourselves that we are thus or thus. Our bodies are our gardens, to the which our wills are gardeners; so that if we will plant nettles or sow lettuce, set hyssop and weed up 323 thyme, supply it with one gender of herbs or distract it with many — either to have it sterile with idleness or manured with industry — why, the power and corrigible authority of this lies in our 327 wills. If the balance of our lives had not one scale of reason to poise another of sensuality, the blood 329 and baseness of our natures would conduct us to most preposterous conclusions. But we have reason to cool our raging motions, our carnal stings, our 332 unbitted lusts; whereof I take this that you call love 333 to be a sect or scion. 334

Roderigo. It cannot be.

Iago. It is merely a lust of the blood and a permission of the will. Come, be a man! Drown thyself? Drown cats and blind puppies! I have professed me thy friend, and I confess me knit to thy deserving with cables of perdurable toughness. I could never better stead thee than now. Put money in thy purse. Follow these wars; defeat thy favor with an 342 usurped beard. I say, put money in thy purse. It cannot be that Desdemona should long continue her love for the Moor — put money in thy purse — nor he his to her. It was a violent commencement, and thou shalt see an answerable sequestration — put 347 but money in thy purse. These Moors are changeable in their wills — fill thy purse with money. The food that to him now is as luscious as locusts shall be to him shortly as bitter as coloquintida. She 351 must change for youth: when she is sated with his body, she will find the error of her choice. (She must have change, she must.) Therefore put money in thy purse. If thou wilt needs damn thyself, do it a more delicate way than drowning. Make all the 356 money thou canst. If sanctimony and a frail vow betwixt an erring barbarian and a supersubtle Ve- 358 netian be not too hard for my wits and all the tribe of hell, thou shalt enjoy her. Therefore make money. A pox of drowning! 'Tis clean out of the way. Seek thou rather to be hanged in compassing thy joy than to be drowned and go without her.

Roderigo. Wilt thou be fast to my hopes, if I depend on the issue?

Iago. Thou art sure of me. Go, make money. I have told thee often, and I retell thee again and again, I hate the Moor. My cause is hearted; thine 368 hath no less reason. Let us be conjunctive in our

323. "hyssop": fragrant herb.

327. "corrigible authority": corrective power.

329. "poise": counterbalance.
329-30. "blood and baseness": animal instincts.

332-33. "motions": appetites. "unbitted": uncontrolled.

334. "sect or scion": cutting or off-shoot.

342. "defeat thy favor": spoil your appearance.

347. "sequestration": separation.

351. "coloquintida": a bitter fruit.

356. "Make": Get hold of.

358. "erring": wandering.

368. "hearted": heart-felt.

OTHELLO

ACT I SCENE III

(a "violent commencement"); Moors are well known for turning from one desire to another, so that Othello's love for his wife will not last long. He introduces the image of food to make this last point (348-50), additional proof that love, for him, relates solely to the sensitive appetite, to lust. As for Desdemona, he is sure that "She must change for youth" (352), once she is "sated of his body." The student will not have ignored how, throughout this speech, "put money in thy purse" becomes a refrain. The final lines (361-63) underscore the preeminence of will over reason in Iago's philosophy. That he himself is passion's slave is emphasized by his expression of utter hatred and desire for revenge in his next speech. Before Roderigo leaves, he assures Iago that he has been convinced. And, alone on the stage, the villain cynically remarks: "Thus do I ever make my fool my purse..."

In the self-revealing soliloquy with which this act ends, Iago introduces a second motive for his hatred of the Moor and his desire for revenge: he has heard rumors that Othello has had an affair with his wife. For him "mere suspicion . . . Will do for surety" (391-92). It need hardly be pointed out that here speaks a man whose mind, as we have learned already, is poisoned. There is not the slightest evidence in the play that what he chooses to believe is true.

Iago next reveals his immediate plan. Aware that he is esteemed by Othello he will move against the man who trusts him by seeing to it that the Moor will be made to believe that Cassio "is too familiar with his wife" (398). Cassio, he is sure, is just the one who is "framed to make women false" (400) — a tacit tribute to the lieutenant's courtly manners, among other things. The plan seems feasible enough, for the Moor "is of a free and open nature," one who "thinks men honest that but seem to be so . . ." (402). In these two lines Iago gives us much that serves to render probable the subsequent change in the character of Othello: The Moor is prominent among those who place full trust in the ensign; he is the man who admitted that he knew "little of this great world . . . More than pertains to feats of broils and battle" (I.iii.86-7). In the final couplet which contains the reference to "Hell and night" (the latter term standing for chaos as opposed to order) and to "monstrous birth" (signifying the unnaturalness of what Iago plans) the diabolic element in the ensign's character is stressed for a second time.

revenge against him. If thou canst cuckold him, thou dost thyself a pleasure, me a sport. There are many events in the womb of time, which will be delivered. Traverse, go, provide thy money! 373
We will have more of this to-morrow. Adieu.
   Roderigo. Where shall we meet i' th' morning?
   Iago. At my lodging.
   Roderigo. I'll be with thee betimes. 377
   Iago. Go to, farewell. — Do you hear, Roderigo?
   Roderigo. What say you?
   Iago. No more of drowning, do you hear?
   Roderigo. I am changed.
   Iago. Go to, farewell. Put money enough in
    your purse.
   Roderigo. I'll sell all my land.   *[Exit.*
   Iago. Thus do I ever make my fool my purse;
For I mine own gained knowledge should profane
If I would time expend with such a snipe 387
But for my sport and profit. I hate the Moor;
And it is thought abroad that 'twixt my sheets
H'as done my office. I know not if't be true;
Yet I, for mere suspicion in that kind,
Will do as if for surety. He holds me well; 392
The better shall my purpose work on him.
Cassio's a proper man. Let me see now; 394
To get his place, and to plume up my will 395
In double knavery — How, how? — Let's see: —
After some time, to abuse Othello's ear
That he is too familiar with his wife.
He hath a person and a smooth dispose 399
To be suspected — framed to make women false.
The Moor is of a free and open nature 401
That thinks men honest that but seem to be so;
And will as tenderly be led by th' nose
As asses are.
I have't! It is engendered! Hell and night 405
Must bring this monstrous birth to the world's
   light.   *[Exit.*

373. "Traverse": forward.

377. "betimes": early.

387. "snipe": woodcock, a ridiculous bird.

392. "well": in high esteem.

394. "proper": handsome.

395. "plume up': gratify.

399. "dispose": disposition.

401. "free": frank.

405. "engendered": conceived.

ACT TWO, scene one.

(A Seaport in Cyprus)

Enter Montano *and two* Gentlemen.

Montano. What from the cape can you discern
  at sea?
1. Gentleman. Nothing at all: it is a high-wrought
  flood.   2
I cannot 'twixt the heaven and the main
Descry sail.
  Montano. Methinks the wind hath spoke aloud at
  land;
A fuller blast ne'er shook our battlements.
If it hath ruffianed so upon the sea,
What ribs of oak, when mountains melt on them,
Can hold the mortise? What shall we hear of this?   9
  2. Gentleman. A segregation of the Turkish fleet.   10
For do but stand upon the foaming shore,
The chidden billow seems to pelt the clouds;
The wind-shaked surge, with high and monstrous
  mane,
Seems to cast water on the burning Bear   14
And quench the Guards of th' ever-fixed pole.   15
I never did like molestation view   16
On the enchafed flood.
  Montano.   If that the Turkish fleet   17
Be not ensheltered and embayed, they are drowned;
It is impossible they bear it out.

Enter a third Gentleman.

3. Gentleman. News, lads! Our wars are done.
The desperate tempest hath so banged the Turks
That their designment halts. A noble ship of Venice   22
Has seen a grievous wrack and sufferance   23
On most part of their fleet.
  Montano. How? Is this true?
  3. Gentleman.   The ship is here put in,
A Veronesa; Michael Cassio,   26
Lieutenant to the warlike Moor Othello,
Is come on shore; the Moor himself at sea,
And is in full commission here for Cyprus.   29
  Montano. I am glad on't. 'Tis a worthy governor.
  3. Gentleman. But this same Cassio, though he
  speak of comfort
Touching the Turkish loss, yet he looks sadly
And prays the Moor be safe, for they were parted
With foul and violent tempest.
  Montano.   Pray heaven he be;
For I have served him, and the man commands
Like a full soldier. Let's to the seaside, ho!
As well to see the vessel that's come in
As to throw out our eyes for brave Othello,
Even till we make the main and th' aerial blue

An indistinct regard.
    3. Gentleman.   Come, let's do so;   40
For every minute is expectancy
Of more arrivance.

Enter CASSIO.

Cassio. Thanks, you the valiant of this warlike isle,
That so approve the Moor! O, let the heavens
Give him defense against the elements,
For I have lost him on a dangerous sea!
    Montano. Is he well shipped?
    Cassio. His bark is stoutly timbered, and his pilot
Of very expert and approved allowance;   49
Therefore my hopes, not surfeited to death,   50
Stand in bold cure.   [*Within*] A sail, a sail, a sail!   51

Enter a Messenger.

Cassio. What noise?
Messenger. The town is empty; on the brow o' th'
    sea
Stand ranks of people, and they cry 'A sail!'
Cassio. My hopes do shape him for the governor.
                        [*A shot.*
2. Gentleman. They do discharge their shot of
    courtesy:
Our friends at least.
    Cassio.   I pray you, sir, go forth
And give us truth who 'tis that is arrived.
    2. Gentleman. I shall.   [*Exit.*
    Montano. But, good lieutenant, is your general
    wived?
    Cassio. Most fortunately. He hath achieved a maid   61
That paragons description and wild fame;   62
One that excels the quirks of blazoning pens,   63
And in th' essential vesture of creation   64
Does tire the ingener.

Enter Second Gentleman.

                 How now? Who has put in?   65
    2. Gentleman. 'Tis one Iago, ancient to the general.
    Cassio. H'as had most favorable and happy speed:
Tempests themselves, high seas, and howling winds,
The guttered rocks and congregated sands,   69
Traitors ensteeped to clog the guiltless keel   70
As having sense of beauty, do omit
Their mortal natures, letting go safely by   72
The divine Desdemona.
    Montano.   What is she?
    Cassio. She that I spake of, our great captain's
    captain,
Left in the conduct of the bold Iago,   75
Whose footing here anticipates our thoughts   76
A se'nnight's speed. Great Jove, Othello guard,   77
And swell his sail with thine own pow'rful breath,
That he may bless this bay with his tall ship,
Make love's quick pants in Desdemona's arms,

But it is not Othello's ship; rather it is the one bearing Desdemona, Iago, and other members of her entourage. The way is prepared for the young lady's entrance in the brief dialogue between Cassio and Montano. Anticipating his repeated use of superlatives, the lieutenant describes her as a maid who surpasses "description and wild fame" (61-2). To him she is the "divine Desdemona" (73) and the "great captain's captain" (74). Once more Cassio voices a prayer for the safety of his commanding officer: may he soon be reunited with his fair bride. What is significant here, a point not to be missed in view of Cassio's demonstration of gallantry which follows shortly, is that the lieutenant remains an honorable man, one who could not betray the Moor.

---

40. "an indistinct regard": indistinguishable.

49. "approved allowance": tested repute.
50. "surfeited to death": overindulged.
51. "in bold cure": an excellent chance of fulfillment.

61. "achieved": won.
62. "paragons": surpasses.
63. "quirks": ingenuities. "blazoning": describing.
64-65. "And . . . ingener": in her superior beauty puts such a strain upon the artist that he exhausts himself.

69. "guttered": jagged.
70. "ensteeped": submerged.

72. "mortal": deadly.

75. "conduct": escort.
76. "footing": landing.
77. "se'nnight's": week's.

Desdemona now appears with Roderigo and Emilia, whom we meet for the first time. Cassio hails her as if she were one to be venerated like the Virgin Mary. She is the "riches of the ship" (83) and "the grace of heaven" to whom all must pay their respects by kneeling. As for this paragon, the lady herself, she briefly thanks Cassio and immediately inquires about her husband. It may be pointed out here and now that throughout the subsequent action up to the arrival of Othello, his well-being remains her deep concern, despite the frivolous dialogue with "honest" Iago.

Give renewed fire to our extinct spirits,   81
(And bring all Cyprus comfort!)

Enter DESDEMONA, IAGO, RODERIGO, *and* EMILIA
with Attendants.

        O, behold!
The riches of the ship is come on shore!
Ye men of Cyprus, let her have your knees.
Hail to thee, lady! and the grace of heaven,
Before, behind thee, and on every hand,
Enwheel thee round!

Desdemona.   I thank you, valiant Cassio.   87
What tidings can you tell me of my lord?

Cassio. He is not yet arrived; nor know I aught
But that he's well and will be shortly here.

Desdemona. O but I fear! How lost you company?

Cassio. The great contention of the sea and skies
Parted our fellowship. [*Within*] A sail, a sail!
                     [*A shot.*
       But hark. A sail!

2. Gentleman. They give their greeting to the
    citadel;
This likewise is a friend.

Cassio.   See for the news.
               [*Exit* Gentlemen.
Good ancient, you are welcome. [*to* EMILIA] Welcome, mistress. —
Let it not gall your patience, good Iago,
That I extend my manners. 'Tis my breeding   98
That gives me this bold show of courtesy.
              [*Kisses* EMILIA. S.D.

Iago. Sir, would she give you so much of her lips
As of her tongue she oft bestows on me,
You would have enough.

Desdemona.   Alas, she has no speech!

Iago. In faith, too much.
I find it still when I have list to sleep.   104
Marry, before your ladyship, I grant,
She puts her tongue a little in her heart
And chides with thinking.   107

Emilia. You have little cause to say so.

Iago. Come on, come on! You are pictures out
    of doors.   109
Bells in your parlors, wildcats in your kitchen,
Saints in your injuries, devils being offended,   111
Players in your housewifery, and housewives in
    your beds.   112

Desdemona. O, fie upon thee, slanderer!

Iago. Nay, it is true, or else I am a Turk:
You rise to play, and go to bed to work.

Emilia. You shall not write my praise.

Iago.   No, let me not.

Desdemona. What wouldst thou write of me, if thou
    shouldest praise me?

Iago. O gentle lady, do not put me to't,
For I am nothing if not critical.

Desdemona. Come on, assay. — There's one gone
    to the harbor?   120

81. "extincted": extinguished.

87. "enwheel": encompass.

98. "extend my manners": greet your wife in this fashion.

S.D. "Kisses Emilia": the usual Renaissance form of social courtesy.

104. "list": desire.

107. "with thinking": without words.

109. "pictures": painted creatures.

111. "saints . . . injuries": offend sanctimoniously.

112. "housewifery": housekeeping. "housewives": hussies.

120. "assay": try.

OTHELLO

ACT II SCENE 1

A third ship is sighted, and while all await its arrival in port, the amenities are taken care of. Cassio, a Florentine — that is, the native of a city whose inhabitants were famous for their courtly manners —, welcomes Emilia with a kiss, a common form of social courtesy at the time. Two things are to be noted here: first, Emilia must be young and attractive enough to attract the harmless gallantry of Cassio (her husband, we know, was in his late twenties) and thus give Iago some excuse for believing that she may be unfaithful; second, the ensign is given the opportunity to introduce the satirical anti-feminine theme which he develops comically but often coarsely in his subsequent dialogue with Desdemona. His attitude toward love of man and woman we know already to be a completely cynical one.

In his discourse Iago indeed emerges as "most profane and liberal (licentious) counselor as Desdemona says (164). Some critics, beginning with Thomas Rymer (Short View of Tragedy, 1692) have been disturbed by this part of the scene. Why, they ask, should Desdemona, "a maiden never bold," indulge in such a colloquy and manifest such apparent gaiety? In reply, one should recognize that Desdemona, as a well-born, well-educated daughter of a Venetian senator, had been trained to adapt herself easily in any social situation. And she will demonstrate this talent later in the play. Here she chooses to indulge one who, it would seem, essays the role of a privileged court jester whose function is to amuse those present in his own often impertinent manner. So Desdemona maintains her position with complete poise. Never does she lose her prime concern for the welfare of her husband, as lines 120-124 made abundantly clear. As for Iago, he knows exactly how far he can approach the obscene without offending his listeners. And, to be sure, there is Cassio to come to his defense (165-6) so that he appears to be the manly, plain-spoken soldier who provides a contrast to the courtly lieutenant.

Iago's aside, spoken as he observes Cassio's behavior in relation to Desdemona (167-178), is as revealing of his character as is any one of his soliloquies. He interprets the gallantry of the lieutenant as evidence of gross sensuality, the sight of which gives him abnormal satisfaction. All this is consistent with what we have learned about him in Act I. Even more important is the fact that he tells us in so many words how he will capitalize on Cassio's good manners.

Iago. Ay, madam.

Desdemona. I am not merry; but I do beguile
The thing I am by seeming otherwise. —
Come, how wouldst thou praise me?

Iago. I am about it; but indeed my invention
Comes from my pate as birdlime does from frieze — 126
It plucks out brains and all. But my Muse labors,
And thus she is delivered:
If she be fair and wise, fairness and wit —
The one's for use, the other useth it.

Desdemona. Well praised! How if she be black
    and witty? 131

Iago. If she be black, and thereto have a wit,
She'll find a white that shall her blackness fit. 133

Desdemona. Worse and worse!

Emilia. How if fair and foolish?

Iago. She never yet was foolish that was fair,
For even her folly helped her to an heir. 137

Desdemona. These are old fond paradoxes to make 138
fools laugh i' th' alehouse. What miserable praise
hast thou for her that's foul and foolish?

Iago. There's none so foul, and foolish thereunto,
But does foul pranks which fair and wise ones do.

Desdemona. O heavy ignorance! Thou praisest the worst best. But what praise couldst thou bestow on a deserving woman indeed — one that in the authority of her merit did justly put on the vouch 146
of very malice itself?

Iago. She that was ever fair, and never proud;
Had tongue at will, and yet was never loud;
Never lacked gold, and yet went never gay;
Fled from her wish, and yet said 'Now I may';
She that, being angered, her revenge being nigh,
Bade her wrong stay, and her displeasure fly;
She that in wisdom never was so frail
To change the cod's head for the salmon's tail; 155
She that could think, and ne'er disclose her mind;
See suitors following, and not look behind:
She was a wight (if ever such wight were) —

Desdemona. To do what?

Iago. To suckle fools and chronicle small beer. 160

Desdemona. O most lame and impotent conclusion! Do not learn of him, Emilia, though he be thy husband. How say you, Cassio? Is he not a most profane and liberal counsellor? 164

Cassio. He speaks home, madam. You may relish 165
him more in the soldier than in the scholar.

Iago. [aside] He takes her by the palm. Ay, well 167
said, whisper! With as little a web as this will I ensnare as great a fly as Cassio. Ay, smile upon her, do! I will gyve thee in thine own courtship. — You 170
say true; 'tis so, indeed! If such tricks as these strip you out of your lieutenantry, it had been better you had not kissed your three fingers so oft — which now again you are most apt to play the sir in. Very 174
good! well kissed! an excellent curtsy! 'Tis so, indeed. 175
deed. Yet again your fingers to your lips? Would they were clyster pipes for your sake! [*Trumpet* 177
within.] The Moor! I know his trumpet.

126. "birdlime": a kind of paste. "frieze": rough cloth.

131. "black": brunette.

133. "white": a pun on wight, meaning "person."

137. "folly": wantonness.
138. "fond": ugly.

146. "put on the vouch": force the approval.

155. "To . . . tail": to take the worthless in exchange for the valuable.

160. "chronicle small beer": to keep petty accounts.

164. "profane . . . counsellor": worldly and licentious.
165. "home": bluntly.

167. "well said": well done.

170. "gyve . . . courtship": fetter you by means of your own courtly behavior.

174. "sir": courtly gentleman.
175. "curtsy": courtesy.

177. "clyster pipes": syringes.

OTHELLO

Othello and his attendants arrive, and the mood changes as he exchanges affectionate greetings with Desdemona, his "fair warrior." It is the Moor, as a great poet, who speaks here (183-199) in lines weighty with import as regards the understanding of the entire action in the play. Storms in the mature Shakespeare tend to be symbolic (Cf. those in King Lear, Macbeth, and The Tempest). The protagonist has arrived safely after experiencing a terrifying tempest at sea, and he describes it in lines the very cadence of which conveys the turbulence during that great storm. (See particularly lines 187-9). Note the simile "as hell's from heaven!" This is another example of dramatic presaging, and so with reference to the Moor's use of the word fear (190). He has passed safely through a kind of hell, one involving great physical danger; he is to experience another kind of hell, one relating to his very soul. Othello indeed is in paradise, a metaphor not inappropriate, especially in view of the religious tone with which this passage ends: Desdemona's prayer to the heavens (193-5) and Othello's fervent "amen" to that prayer.

No one will have missed the significance of Iago's aside (199-201) as he observes all this. His metaphor from music is the correct one to convey his intentions, to destroy the Moor; for music, representing harmony, was a familiar figure of speech used to develop the concept of order as opposed to chaos — the natural as opposed to the unnatural.

Othello next announces the good news: "Our wars are done; the Turks are drowned" (202), courteously addressing Montano as an "old acquaintance" whom he esteems highly. But he devotes most of his lines to another expression of his love for Desdemona (204-12). And in this speech he repeats his belief that Iago is completely trustworthy.

The villain and Roderigo find themselves together again on stage, and the medium shifts to prose. Iago then proceeds to provide the gull with an interpretation of what both have seen and to tell him what must be done now. All Roderigo has to do, says Iago in effect, is to exhibit the valiantry which even unworthy men demonstrate when they are in love.

Cassio. 'Tis truly so.
Desdemona. Let's meet him and receive him.
Cassio. Lo, where he comes.

Enter OTHELLO *and* Attendants.

Othello. O my fair warrior!
Desdemona.   My dear Othello!
Othello. It gives me wonder great as my content
To see you here before me. O my soul's joy!
If after every tempest come such calms,
May the winds blow till they have wakened death!
And let the laboring bark climb hills of seas
Olympus-high, and duck again so low
As hell's from heaven! If it were now to die,
'Twere now to be most happy; for I fear
My soul hath her content so absolute
That not another comfort like to this
Succeeds in unknown fate.
Desdemona.   The heavens forbid
But that our loves and comforts should increase
Even as our days grow.
Othello.   Amen to that, sweet powers!
I cannot speak enough of this content;
It stops me here; it is too much of joy.   197
And this, and this, the greatest discords be
                              [*They kiss.*
That e'er our hearts shall make!
Iago.   [*aside*] O, you are well tuned now!

But I'll set down the pegs that make this music,   200
As honest as I am.
Othello.   Come, let us to the castle.
News, friends! Our wars are done; the Turks are
     drowned.
How does my old acquaintance of this isle? —
Honey, you shall be well desired in Cyprus;   204
I have found a great love amongst them. O my sweet,
I prattle out of fashion, and I dote   206
In mine own comforts, I prithee, good Iago,
Go to the bay and disembark my coffers.   208
Bring thou the master to the citadel;   209
He is a good one, and his worthiness
Does challenge much respect. — Come Desdemona,   211
Once more well met at Cyprus.

[*Exit* OTHELLO *with all but* IAGO *and* RODERIGO.

Iago. [*to an Attendant, who goes out*] Do thou
meet me presently at the harbor [*to* RODERIGO] 214
Come hither. If thou be'st valiant (as they say base
men being in love have then a nobility in their natures more than is native to them), list me. The
lieutenant to-night watches on the court of guard. 218
First, I must tell thee this: Desdemona is directly
in love with him.
Roderigo. With him? Why, 'tis not possible.
Iago. Lay thy finger thus, and let thy soul be in- 222
structed. Mark me with what violence she first

197. "here": in my heart.

200. "set down": loosen (i.e., make one sing a different tune.)

204. "well desired": warmly greeted.

206. "prattle . . . fashion": talk idly.

208. "coffers": trunks.

209. "master": ship captain.

211. "challenge": claim.

214. "presently": immediately.

218. "court of guard": headquarters.

222. "thus": on the lips.

36

ACT II SCENE I

(The irony here is only too apparent.) The villain then flatly states that Cassio unmistakably is in love with Desdemona. Roderigo finds this to be impossible, but the ensign easily convinces him that such is the case. First he provides the groundwork for supporting his indictment: the "violence" with which she first loved the Moor (223), who won her with his "bragging" and his "fantastical lies"; she will tire of his "prating" in due time. And, once more exhibiting his concept of love as being no more than lust, Iago assures Roderigo that the lady will satisfy her physical appetite soon enough and will look for a man who, in contrast to Othello, will be youthfully attractive. "Very nature will instruct her in it and compel a second choice" (235-6). Not without interest is Iago's view of what is natural as opposed to that of the protagonist and of all the sympathetic characters in this play. The villain's utter coarseness is especially indicated when he assures his dupe that the delicate Desdemona will "begin to heave the gorge, disrelish and abhor the Moor." (234-35). The image, with its stress on physical appetite and nausea, is typical of the man.

The ensign then disposes of the courtly Cassio contemptuously. He repeatedly refers to the lieutenant as a knave, a slippery and subtle, even devilish one. Again Roderigo cannot believe for he cannot believe that Desdemona would be attracted to such a man — she, a woman of "blessed" character. Iago seizes upon the adjective scornfully. Desdemona, he says in effect, is human enough and therefore prone to err. Did not Roderigo himself see how she did "paddle with the palm of [Cassio's] hand?" A sure sign of lechery this, not a matter of courtesy as Roderigo believed. It was, the ensign concludes, a "prologue to the history of lust and foul thoughts" (261-2).

Now for Iago's plan. This very night Roderigo must find some excuse to anger the lieutenant. But yet again the gull is dubious: Cassio had appeared to him as a man fully in control of his passions. Iago assures him that Cassio is nothing of the sort, that he is a man with a violent temper. Let Roderigo provoke him and make him lose control of himself; then will the young Venetian find "a shorter journey to [his] desires" (281). Roderigo agrees to carry through with this plan, and he leaves the stage, giving his mentor another chance to soliloquize.

loved the Moor, but for bragging and telling her 224
fantastical lies; and will she love him still for prating? Let not thy discreet heart think it. Her eye must be fed; and what delight shall she have to look on the devil? When the blood is made dull with the act of sport, there should be, again to inflame it and to give satiety a fresh appetite, loveliness in favor, sympathy in years, manners, and 231 beauties; all which the Moor is defective in. Now for want of these required conveniences, her delicate 233 tenderness will find itself abused, begin to heave the 234 gorge, disrelish and abhor the Moor. Very nature 235 will instruct her in it and compel her to some second choice. Now, sir, this granted — as it is a most pregnant and unforced position — who stands 238 so eminent in the degree of this fortune as Cassio does? A knave very voluble; no further conscionable 240 than in putting on the mere form of civil and hu- 241 mane seeming for the better compassing of his salt 242 and most hidden loose affections? Why, none! Why, none! A slipper and subtle knave; a finder-out of 244 occasions; that has an eye can stamp and counter- 245 feit advantages, though true advantage never pre- 246 sent itself; a devilish knave! Besides, the knave is handsome, young, and hath all those requisites in him that folly and green minds look after. A pestilent complete knave! and the woman hath found him already.

Roderigo. I cannot believe that in her; she's full of most blessed condition. 253

Iago. Blessed fig's-end! The wine she drinks is made of grapes. If she had been blessed, she would never have loved the Moor. Blessed pudding! Didst thou not see her paddle with the palm of his hand? Didst not mark that?

Roderigo. Yes, that I did; but that was but courtesy.

Iago. Lechery, by this hand! an index and obscure prologue to the history of lust and foul thoughts. They met so near with their lips that their breaths embraced together. Villainous thoughts, Roderigo! When these mutualities so marshal the 264 way, hard at hand comes the master and main exercise, th' incorporate conclusion. Pish! But, sir, 266 be you ruled by me: I have brought you from Venice. Watch you to-night; for the command, I'll lay't upon you. Cassio knows you not. I'll not be far from you: do you find some occasion to anger Cassio, either by speaking too loud, or tainting his 271 discipline, or from what other course you please which the time shall more favorably minister.

Roderigo. Well.

Iago. Sir, he is rash and very sudden in choler, and 275 haply with his truncheon may strike at you. Provoke him that he may; for even out of that will I cause these of Cyprus to mutiny; whose qualifica- 278 tion shall come into no true taste again but the displanting of Cassio. So shall you have a shorter journey to your desires by the means I shall then have to prefer them; and the impediment most 282

224. "but for": only for.

231. "favor": face.

233. "conveniences": compatibilities.
234. "heave the gorge": become nauseated.

238. "pregnant": most significant.

240. "conscionable": conscientious.
241. "humane seeming": courteous appearance.
242. "salt": lecherous.

244. "slipper": slippery.
245-46. "can . . . advantages": forge false opportunities.

253. "condition": disposition.

264. "mutualities": exchanges.

266. "incorporate": carnal.

271. "tainting": discrediting.

275. "sudden in choler": violent in anger.

278. "qualification": appeasement.
"true taste": satisfactory state.

282. "prefer": advance.

OTHELLO

ACT II SCENE I

The villain first assures himself (and the audience) that he has no doubts regarding Cassio's attitude toward Desdemona and that it is highly probable that she loves the lieutenant. Yet, and here is the testimony of a hostile witness, he concedes that Othello "Is of a constant, loving nature" (293), one who will prove "to Desdemona A most dear husband" (294-5). It comes as a surprise to hear him say that he too loves the young lady, but then he explains: it is not a matter of lust on his part but a desire to avenge himself; and he voices for the second time his conviction that the Moor has had a love affair with Emilia, concluding that he will get even "wife for wife." The earlier comment as regards Iago's belief makes any additional comment unnecessary.

Roderigo, whom Iago refers to as "this poor trash of Venice" (307), will, the villain is sure, make it possible for him to have at his mercy Cassio, the man also suspected of having an illicit affair with the maligned Emilia. Then, concludes Iago, he will win the thanks and regard of Othello, whom he will mislead to achieve his primary purpose. "'Tis here, but yet confused," he adds (315) — plain evidence that from the start he has been an improviser in his villainy. He will not delay, we are assured in the closing line.

ACT II SCENE II

This scene, occasionally combined with the one that follows, serves in the same way as a curtain in a modern theater, indicating a passage of time. Shakespeare is exact in telling the hour involved (11). Notice how the epithets "noble" and "valiant" continue to be applied to Othello.

---

profitably removed without the which there were no expectation of our prosperity.

Roderigo. I will do this if you can bring it to any opportunity.

Iago. I warrant thee. Meet me by and by at the citadel; I must fetch his necessaries ashore. Farewell.

Roderigo. Adieu. [*Exit.*

Iago. That Cassio loves her, I do well believe it;
That she loves him, 'tis apt and of great credit. 291
The Moor, howbeit that I endure him not,
Is of a constant, loving, noble nature,
And I dare think he'll prove to Desdemona
A most dear husband. Now I do love her too;
Not out of absolute lust, though peradventure
I stand accountant for as great a sin, 297
But partly led to diet my revenge,
For that I do suspect the lusty Moor
Hath leaped into my seat; the thought whereof
Doth, like a poisonous mineral, gnaw my inwards;
And nothing can or shall content my soul
Till I am evened with him, wife for wife:
Or failing so, yet that I put the Moor
At least into a jealousy so strong
That judgment cannot cure. Which thing to do,
If this poor trash of Venice, whom I trash
For his quick hunting, stand the putting on, 308
I'll have our Michael Cassio on the hip, 309
Abuse him to the Moor in the rank garb 310
(For I fear Cassio with my nightcap too),
Make the Moor thank me, love me, and reward me
For making him egregiously an ass
And practicing upon his peace and quiet 314
Even to madness. 'Tis here, but yet confused:
Knavery's plain face is never seen till used. [*Exit.*

---

291. "apt": probable.

297. "accountant": accountable.

308. "For": in order to develop.
"stand ... on": respond to my inciting.
309. "on the hip": at my mercy.
310. "rank garb": gross manner.

314. "practicing upon": plotting against.

Scene two.

(A STREET)

Enter OTHELLO'S HERALD, *with a proclamation.*

Herald. It is Othello's pleasure, our noble and valiant general, that, upon certain tidings now arrived, importing the mere perdition of the Turkish fleet, 3
every man put himself into triumph; some to dance, some to make bonfires, each man to what sport and revels his addiction leads him. For, besides these 6
beneficial news, it is the celebration of his nuptial. So much was his pleasure should be proclaimed. All offices are open, and there is full liberty of feasting 9
from this present hour of five till the bell have told eleven. Heaven bless the isle of Cyprus and our noble general Othello! [*Exit.*

3. "mere perdition": complete destruction.

6. "addiction": inclination.

9. "offices": kitchens and storerooms.

Othello, Desdemona, Cassio, and attendants enter a hall in the castle. The Moor instructs "good Michael" to inspect the guard during the night. His brief counsel deserves attention in view of the subsequent change in both Cassio and the general himself. Both are men who do not "outsport discretion" at this point in the action. When Cassio states that Iago has been given proper instructions, Othello is satisfied: "Iago is most honest."

In lines 9-11, addressed to Desdemona, Othello does make reference to the consummation of their love, but that love remains rational for the two, despite the commercial metaphor ("purchases") which the Moor uses. It is Iago, appearing in the company of Cassio, who provides a carnal interpretation of the relationship of bride and groom (13-24). Cassio, gentleman that he is, refuses to descend to this level. To him Desdemona remains "a most exquisite lady" who "is indeed perfection."

In the spirit of what appears to be no more than manly good fellowship, Iago invites the lieutenant to join him and two Cyprians in drinking wine "to the health of black Othello" (28-9). When Cassio begs off, explaining that he has "very poor and unhappy brains for drinking" and has already had a single measure of wine, Iago is only the more insistent, basing his argument on the demands of friendship and the nature of the occasion. With misgivings Cassio leaves to call in the gallants, and in soliloquy Iago reveals his plan: already he has seen to it that Roderigo and guardsmen have imbibed sufficiently; if he can induce Cassio to drink wine he is sure that the lieutenant will lose control of himself.

Scene three.

(A HALL IN THE CASTLE)

Enter OTHELLO, DESDEMONA, CASSIO, *and* Attendants.

Othello. Good Michael, look you to the guard to-night.
Let's teach ourselves that honorable stop,
Not to outsport discretion.
Cassio. Iago hath direction what to do;
But not withstanding, with my personal eye
Will I look to't.
Othello. Iago is most honest.
Michael, good night. To-morrow with your earliest   7
Let me have speech with you. [*to* DESDEMONA]
    Come, my dear love.
The purchase made, the fruits are to ensue;
That profit's yet to come 'tween me and you.
Good night.
    [*Exit* OTHELLO *with* DESDEMONA *and* Attendants.

Enter IAGO.

Cassio. Welcome, Iago. We must to the watch.
Iago. Not this hour, lieutenant; 'tis not yet ten o'   14
th' clock. Our general cast us thus early for the love
of his Desdemona; who let us not therefore blame.
He hath not yet made wanton the night with her, and
she is sport for Jove.
Cassio. She's a most exquisite lady.
Iago. And, I'll warrant her, full of game.
Cassio. Indeed, she's a most fresh and delicate
    creature.
Iago. What an eye she has! Methinks it sounds a   21
parley to provocation.   22
Cassio. An inviting eye; and yet methinks right
    modest.
Iago. And when she speaks, is it not an alarum to
    love?
Cassio. She is indeed perfection.
Iago. Well, happiness to their sheets! Come, lieutenant, I have a stoup of wine, and here without are   27
a brace of Cyprus gallants that would fain have a
measure to the health of black Othello.
Cassio. Not to-night, good Iago. I have very poor
and unhappy brains for drinking; I could well wish
courtesy would invent some other custom of entertainment.
Iago. O, they are our friends. But one cup! I'll
drink for you.
Cassio. I have drunk but one cup to-night, and that
was craftily qualified too; and behold what innova-   37
tion it makes here. I am unfortunate in the infirmity
and dare not task my weakness with any more.
Iago. What, man! 'Tis a night of revels: the gallants desire it.

---

7. "with your earliest": very early.

14. "cast": dismissed.

21 "sounds . . . provocation": leads to talk of love.

27. "stoup": two-quart tankard.

37. "craftily qualified": slyly diluted by Cassio, himself.

The drinking episode that follows is a good lively one. Montano has joined the group. Iago sets the tone with his drinking songs, playing to perfection the role of the hail-fellow-well-met. Cassio does become drunk, his speech thick, his physical actions uncertain. He insists that he is sober and all good-naturedly agree with him as he staggers from the stage. This is Iago's first successful trick. Nor is the skill with which he has executed it and with which he immediately begins to follow through with his plan to discredit Cassio to be underestimated. He knew his man well enough to capitalize on one of the man's virtues, for it was out of courtesy that the lieutenant had been led to imbibe, despite his self-admitted weakness.

Cassio. Where are they?

Iago. Here at the door; I pray you call them in.

Cassio. I'll do't, but it dislikes me.   [*Exit.* 44

Iago. If I can fasten but one cup upon him
With that which he hath drunk to-night already,
He'll be as full of quarrel and offense
As my young mistress' dog. Now my sick fool Roderigo,
Whom love hath turned almost the wrong side out,
To Desdemona hath to-night caroused   50
Potations pottle-deep; and he's to watch.   51
Three lads of Cyprus — Noble swelling spirits,
That hold their honors in a wary distance,   53
The very elements of this warlike isle —   54
Have I to-night flustered with flowing cups,
And they watch too. Now, 'mongst this flock of drunkards
Am I to put our Cassio in some action
That may offend the isle.

Enter CASSIO, MONTANO, *and* Gentlemen; Servants
following with wine.

But here they come.
If consequence do but approve my dream,
My boat sails freely, both with wind and stream.

Cassio. 'Fore God, they have given me a rouse   61
already.

Montano. Good faith, a little one; not past a pint, as I am a soldier.

Iago. Some wine, ho!

[*Sings*] And let me the canakin clink, clink;   66
      And let me the canakin clink.
        A soldier's a man;
        A life's but a span,
      Why then, let a soldier drink.
Some wine, boys!

Cassio. 'Fore God, an excellent song!

Iago. I learned it in England, where indeed they are most potent in potting. Your Dane, your German, and your swag-bellied Hollander — Drink, ho! —   75
are nothing to your English.

Cassio. Is your Englishman so expert in his drinking?

Iago. Why, he drinks you with facility your Dane dead drunk; he sweats not to overthrow your Almain; he gives your Hollander a vomit ere the next   79
pottle can be filled.

Cassio. To the health of our general!

Montano. I am for it, lieutenant, and I'll do you justice.

Iago. O sweet England!

[*Sings*] King Stephen was a worthy peer;
      His breeches cost him but a crown;
    He held 'em sixpence all too dear,
      With that he called the tailor lown.   88
    He was a wight of high renown,
      And thou art but of low degree.
    'Tis pride that pulls the country down;
      Then take thine auld cloak about thee.

44. "dislikes": displeases.

50. "caroused": drunk healths.

51. "pottle-deep": to the bottom of the tankard.

53. "That . . . distance": most sensitive in the matter of honor.

54. "very elements": true representatives.

61. "rouse": bumper.

66. "canakin": drinking pot.

75. "swag-bellied": loose-bellied.

79. "Almain": German.

88. "lown": rascal.

Iago's lines addressed to Montano (117) well illustrate his ingenuity. He is careful to express high praise of Cassio, and he voices orthodox doctrine when he speaks of the lieutenant's "vice" as being a "just equinox" to his virtues. Of course the villain tells a bare-faced lie when he assures Montano that Cassio is a confirmed drinker. And Montano agrees that the general should be informed. Of special interest is his remark that Othello may prize "the virtue that appears in Cassio" and be unaware of his "evils." There is irony here in the light of later events.

Roderigo makes a brief appearance, staying only to receive instructions: seek out Cassio. Turning again to Montano Iago declares that he would do only that which would help the lieutenant to master his weakness.

An exciting episode follows. Cassio appears in pursuit of the hapless Roderigo, whom he denounces as a rogue and rascal. Montano endeavors to intercede and Cassio turns on him, giving Iago the chance to instruct Roderigo. The dupe is told to raise a general alarm while the ensign himself assumes the role of peacemaker. Othello, accompanied by armed men, arrives to find that Montano has been wounded but retains enough vigor to turn upon Cassio once more. And now in the presence of the general, Iago renews his efforts to stop the fight. "Hold, hold, for shame!" he exclaims, echoing in part Othello's command (159).

Some wine, ho!

Cassio. 'Fore God, this is a more exquisite song than the other.

Iago. Will you hear't again?

Cassio. No, for I hold him to be unworthy of his place that does those things. Well, God's above all; and there be souls must be saved, and there be souls must not be saved.

Iago. It's true, good lieutenant.

Cassio. For mine own part — no offense to the general, nor any man of quality — I hope to be saved. 103

Iago. And so do I too, lieutenant.

Cassio. Ay, but, by your leave, not before me. The lieutenant is to be saved before the ancient. Let's have no more of this; let's to our affairs. — God forgive us our sins! — Gentlemen, let's look to our business. Do not think, gentlemen, I am drunk. This is my ancient; this is my right hand, and this is my left. I am not drunk now. I can stand well enough, and speak well enough.

All. Excellent well!

Cassio. Why, very well then. You must not not think then that I am drunk. [*Exit.*

Montano. To th' platform, masters. Come, let's set the watch 116

Iago. You see this fellow that is gone before.
He is a soldier fit to stand by Caesar
And give direction; and do but see his vice.
'Tis to his virtue a just equinox, 120
The one as long as th' other. 'Tis pity of him.
I fear the trust Othello puts him in,
One some odd time of his infirmity,
Will shake this island.

Montano. But is he often thus?

Iago. 'Tis evermore the prologue to his sleep:
He'll watch the horologe a double set 126
If drink rock not his cradle.

Montano. It were well
The general were put in mind of it.
Perhaps he sees it not, or his good nature
Prizes the virtue that appears in Cassio
And looks not on his evils. Is not this true?

Enter RODERIGO.

Iago. [*aside to him*] How now, Roderigo?
I pray you after the lieutenant, go! [*Exit* RODERIGO.

Montano. And 'tis great pity that the noble Moor
Should hazard such a place as his own second
With one of an ingraft infirmity. 136
It were an honest action to say
So to the Moor.

Iago. Not I, for this fair island!
I do love Cassio well and would do much
To cure him of this evil. [*Within*] Help! help!
But hark! What noise?

Enter CASSIO, *driving in* RODERIGO.

Cassio. Zounds, you rogue! you rascal!

103. "quality": rank.

116. "platform": level area on the ramparts.
"set ... watch": mount the guard.

120. "just equinox": exact equivalent.

126. "watch ... set": remain awake twice around the clock.

136. "ingraft": habitual.

41

When Othello makes inquiries as the reason for "this barbarous brawl," Iago appears as one reluctant to inform against a friend. Nor can the crushed lieutenant or the wounded Montano provide details. The Moor is appalled to find that a "private and domestic quarrel" should take place when the safety of Cyprus should be the concern of all. First hypocritically declaring that he would rather have his tongue cut out than "do offense to Michael Cassio" (212-13) Iago says enough to convince Othello what action he should take. He is particularly concerned that Desdemona should have been aroused. Cassio is stripped of all authority.

Montano. What's the matter, lieutenant?
Cassio.   A knave teach me my duty?
I'll beat the knave into a twiggen bottle.   143
Roderigo. Beat me?
Cassio.   Dost thou prate, rogue?
                      [*Strikes him.*
Montano.   Nay, good lieutenant!
                      [*Stays him.*
Pray, sir, hold your hand.
Cassio.   Let me go, sir,
Or I'll knock you o'er the mazzard.
Montano.   Come, come, you're drunk! 146
Cassio. Drunk?   [*They fight.*
Iago. [*aside to* RODERIGO]Away, I say! Go out
    and cry a mutiny!   [*Exit* RODERIGO.
Nay, good lieutenant. God's will, gentlemen!
Help, ho! — lieutenant — sir — Montano — sir —
Help, masters! — Here's a goodly watch indeed!
                      [*A bell rung.*
Who's that which rings the bell? Diablo, ho!
The town will rise. God's will, lieutenant, hold!
You will be shamed for ever.

Enter OTHELLO *and* Gentlemen *with weapons.*

Othello.   What is the matter here?
Montano. Zounds, I bleed still. I am hurt to the
    death.
He dies!
Othello. Hold for your lives!
Iago. Hold, hold! Lieutenant — sir — Montano —
    gentlemen!
Have you forgot all sense of place and duty?
Hold! The general speaks to you. Hold, hold, for
    shame!
Othello. Why, how now, ho? From whence ariseth
    this?
Are we turned Turks, and to ourselves do that
Which heaven hath forbid the Ottomites?
For Christian shame put by this barbarous brawl!
He that stirs next to carve for his own rage   164
Holds his soul light; he dies upon his motion.
Silence that dreadful bell! It frights the isle
From her propriety. What's the matter, masters? 167
Honest Iago, that looks dead with grieving,
Speak. Who began this? On thy love, I charge thee.
Iago. I do not know. Friends all but now, even
    now,
In quarter, and in terms like bride and groom   171
Devesting them for bed; and then, but now —
As if some planet had unwitted men —
Swords out, and tilting one at other's breast   174
In opposition bloody. I cannot speak
Any beginning to this peevish odds,   176
And would in action glorious I had lost
Those legs that brought me to a part of it!
Othello. How comes it, Michael, you are thus for-
    got?   179
Cassio. I pray you pardon me; I cannot speak.

143. "twiggen": wicker-covered.

146. "mazzard": head.

164. "carve . . . rage": act on his own impulse.

167. "propriety": proper self.

171. "quarter": friendliness.

174. "tilting": thrusting.

176. "peevish odds": silly quarrel.

179. "are . . . forgot": have so forgotten yourself.

Othello. Worthy Montano, you were wont be civil;
The gravity and stillness of your youth   182
The world hath noted, and your name is great
In mouths of wisest censure. What's the matter   184
That you unlace your reputation thus   185
And spend your rich opinion for the name   186
Of a night-brawler? Give me answer to't.
   Montano. Worthy Othello, I am hurt to danger.
Your officer, Iago, can inform you,
While I spare speech, which something now offends
    me,   190
Of all that I do know; nor know I aught
By me that's said or done amiss this night,
Unless self-charity be sometimes a vice,
And to defend ourselves it be a sin
When violence assails us.
   Othello.   Now, by heaven,
My blood begins my safer guides to rule,   196
And passion, having my best judgment collied,   197
Assays to lead the way. If I once stir   198
Or do but lift this arm, the best of you
Shall sink in my rebuke. Give me to know
How this foul rout began, who set it on;
And he that is approved in this offense,   202
Though he had twinned with me, both at a birth,
Shall lose me. What! in a town of war,
Yet wild, the people's hearts brimful of fear,
To manage private and domestic quarrel?   206
In night, and on the court and guard of safety?
'Tis monstrous. Iago, who began't?
   Montano. If partially affined, or leagued in office, 209
Thou dost deliver more or less than truth,
Thou art no soldier.
   Iago.   Touch me not so near.
I had rather have this tongue cut from my mouth
Than it should do offense to Michael Cassio;
Yet I persuade myself, to speak the truth
Shall nothing wrong him. Thus it is, general.
Montano and myself being in speech,
There comes a fellow crying out for help,
And Cassio following him with determined sword
To execute upon him. Sir, this gentleman   219
Steps in to Cassio and entreats his pause.   220
Myself the crying fellow did pursue,
Lest by his clamor — as it so fell out —
The town might fall in fright. He, swift of foot,
Outran my purpose; and I returned the rather
For that I heard the clink and fall of swords,
And Cassio high in oath; which till to-night
I ne'er might say before. When I came back —
For this was brief — I found them close together
At blow and thrust, even as again they were
When you yourself did part them.
More of this matter cannot I report;
But men are men; the best sometimes forget.
Though Cassio did some little wrong to him,
As men in rage strike those that wish them best,
Yet surely Cassio I believe received
From him that fled some strange indignity,

182. "stillness": staid behavior.

184. "censure": judgment.
185. "unlace": undo.
186. "rich opinion": good reputation.

190. "offends": pains.

196. "blood": passion.
197. "collied": darkened.
198. "Assays": tries.

202. "approved": found guilty.

206. "manage": carry on.

209. "partially . . . office": partial because of friendship.

219. "execute": work his will.
220. "entreats his pause": begs him to stop.

Which patience could not pass.
Othello.   I know, Iago,
Thy honesty and love doth mince this matter,
Making it light to Cassio. Cassio, I love thee;
But never more be officer of mine.

Enter DESDEMONA, *attended.*

Look if my gentle love be not raised up!
I'll make thee an example.
Desdemona.   What's the matter?
Othello. All's well now, sweeting; come away to   243
    bed.
[*To* MONTANO] Sir, for your hurts, myself will be
    your surgeon.
Lead him off.   [MONTANO *is led off.*
Iago, look with care about the town
And silence those whom this vile brawl distracted.
Come, Desdemona: 'tis the soldiers' life
To have their balmy slumbers waked with strife.
                [*Exit with all but* IAGO *and* CASSIO.
Iago. What, are you hurt, lieutenant?
Cassio. Ay, past all surgery.
Iago. Marry, God forbid!
Cassio. Reputation, reputation, reputation! O, I
have lost my reputation! I have lost the immortal
part of myself, and what remains is bestial. My
reputation, Iago, my reputation!
Iago. As I am an honest man, I thought you had
received some bodily wound. There is more sense
in that than in reputation. Reputation is an idle
and most false imposition; oft got without merit   260
and lost without deserving. You have lost no reputation at all unless you repute yourself such a loser.
What, man! there are ways to recover the general
again. You are but now cast in his mood — a pun-   264
ishment more in policy than in malice, even so as   265
one would beat his offenseless dog to affright an
imperious lion. Sue to him again, and he's yours.
Cassio. I will rather sue to be despised than to deceive so good a commander with so slight, so
drunken, and so indiscreet an officer. Drunk! and
speak parrot! and squabble! swagger! swear! and   271
discourse fustian with one's own shadow! O thou   272
invisible spirit of wine, if thou hast no name to be
known by, let us call thee devil!
Iago. What was he that you followed with your
sword? What had he done to you?
Cassio. I know not.
Iago. Is't possible?
Cassio. I remember a mass of things, but nothing
distinctly; a quarrel, but nothing wherefore. O God,
that men should put an enemy in their mouths to
steal away their brains! that we should with joy,
pleasance, revel and applause transform ourselves   283
into beasts!
Iago. Why, but you are now well enough. How
came you thus recovered?
Cassio. It hath pleased the devil drunkenness to
give place to the devil wrath. One unperfectness

When the lieutenant bewails the fact that he has now lost his reputation, Iago is ready with facile words of consolation. He assures Cassio that he has only to wait until the Moor is in a better mood to regain his position. But the lieutenant can do nothing but blame himself. Lines 279-84 incorporate the Renaissance moral view of drunkenness. Iago depreciates all this: wine is "a good familiar creature if used well" (302-3). Cassio is thus easily convinced that Iago gives him sound advice and he agrees to ask Desdemona to intercede for him.

243. "sweeting": sweetheart.

260. "imposition": quality imposed by others.

264. "cast . . . mood": dismissed because of his anger.
265. "in policy": i.e., because he must seem to be angry in view of the presence of the Cypriots.

271. "parrot": nonsense.
272. "fustian": bombast.

283. "pleasance": having a good time. "applause": wish to please.

It is little wonder that, having played his part so well, Iago should ask, in soliloquy, "And what's he then that says I play the villain . . ."? Everything has fallen nicely into place for him. He is now sure that, thanks to Desdemona's virtues and the Moor's love for her, his plan will work out well. With characteristic honesty of the Shakespearean villain in soliloquy, however, he cynically identifies his argument as "Divinity of hell" (345) and tells us what his next step will be: to arouse the passion of jealousy in the noble Moor and thus to "enmesh them all."

shows me another, to make me frankly despise myself.

Iago. Come, you are too severe a moraler. As the time, the place, and the condition of this country stands, I could heartily wish this had not so befall'n; but since it is as it is, mend it for your own good.

Cassio. I will ask him for my place again: he shall tell me I am a drunkard! Had I as many mouths as Hydra, such an answer would stop them all. To be now a sensible man, by and by a fool, and presently a beast! O strange! Every inordinate cup is unblest, and the ingredient is a devil.

Iago. Come, come, good wine is a good familiar creature if it be well used. Exclaim no more against it. And, good lieutenant, I think you think I love you.

Cassio. I have well approved it, sir. I drunk!

Iago. You or any man living may be drunk at some time, man. I'll tell you what you shall do. Our general's wife is now the general. I may say so in this respect, for that he hath devoted and given up himself to the contemplation, mark, and denotement of her parts and graces. Confess yourself freely to her; importune her help to put you in your place again. She is of so free, so kind, so apt, so blessed a disposition she holds it a vice in her goodness not to do more than she is requested. This broken joint between you and her husband entreat her to splinter; and my fortunes against any lay worth naming, this crack of your love shall grow stronger than 'twas before.

Cassio. You advise me well.

Iago. I protest, in the sincerity of love and honest kindness.

Cassio. I think it freely; and betimes in the morning will I beseech the virtuous Desdemona to undertake for me. I am desperate of my fortunes if they check me here.

Iago. You are in the right. Good night, lieutenant; I must to the watch.

Cassio. Good night, honest Iago.   [*Exit* CASSIO.

Iago. And what's he then that says I play the villain,
When this advice is free I give and honest,
Probal to thinking, and indeed the course   333
To win the Moor again? For 'tis most easy
Th' inclining Desdemona to subdue   335
In any honest suit; she's framed as fruitful   336
As the free elements. And then for her
To win the Moor — were't to renounce his baptism,
All seals and symbols of redeemed sin —
His soul is so enfettered to her love
That she may make, unmake, do what she list,
Even as her appetite shall play the god
With his weak function. How am I then a villain   343
To counsel Cassio to this parallel course,   344
Directly to his good? Divinity of hell!   345
When devils will the blackest sins put on,   346

298. "Hydra": hundred-headed beast killed by Hercules.

301. "ingredient": contents.

306. "approved": proved.

311. "denotement": careful observation.

317. "splinter": bind with splints.
318. "lay": wager.

326. "I . . . here": I lack faith in my future if my career is stopped short here.

333. "Probal": probable.

335. "subdue": persuade.
336. "fruitful": generous.

343. "function": mental faculties.
344. "parallel": corresponding.
345. "Divinity": Theology.
346. "put on": incite.

Enter Roderigo, who complains bitterly that he has little money left and has been "well cudgelled." He threatens to return to Venice, but Iago has little trouble in pacifying him. Finally, we learn how Iago will make use of Emilia.

They do suggest at first with heavenly shows,   347
As I do now. For whiles this honest fool
Plies Desdemona to repair his fortunes,
And she for him pleads strongly to the Moor,
I'll pour this pestilence into his ear,
That she repeals him for her body's lust;   352
And by how much she strives to do him good,
She shall undo her credit with the Moor.
So will I turn her virtue into pitch,
And out of her own goodness make the net
That shall enmesh them all.

Enter RODERIGO.

                                    How, now Roderigo?
Roderigo. I do follow here in the chase, not like a
hound that hunts, but one that fills up the cry. My 359
money is almost spent; I have been to-night exceed-
ingly well cudgelled; and I think the issue will
be — I shall have so much experience for my pains;
and so, with no money at all, and a little more wit,
return again to Venice.
Iago. How poor are they that have not patience!
What wound did ever heal but by degrees!
Thou know'st we work by wit, and not by witch-
        craft;
And wit depends on dilatory time.
Does't not go well? Cassio hath beaten thee,
And thou by that small hurt hast cashiered Cassio.   370
Though other things grow fair against the sun,
Yet fruits that blossom first will first be ripe.
Content thyself awhile. By the mass, 'tis morning!
Pleasure and action make the hours seem short.
Retire thee; go where thou art billeted.
Away, I say! Thou shalt know more hereafter.
Nay, get thee gone!   [*Exit* RODERIGO.
            Two things are to be done:
My wife must move for Cassio to her mistress;   378
I'll set her on;
Myself the while to draw the Moor apart
And bring him jump when he may Cassio find   381
Soliciting his wife. Ay, that's the way!
Dull not device by coldness and delay.   [*Exit.*

ACT THREE, scene one.

(BEFORE THE CASTLE)

Enter CASSIO *with* Musicians.

Cassio. Masters, play here, I will content your
        pains: 1
Something that's brief; and bid 'Good morrow,
        general.'   [*Music.*

Enter the Clown.

347. "suggest": seduce.

352. "repeals him": seeks his recall.

359. "cry": pack.

370. "cashiered": made possible the discharge of Cassio.

378. "move": petition.

381. "jump": at the precise moment.

1. "content": reward.

OTHELLO

ACT III SCENE I

Cassio has arranged for a group of musicians to play an aubade before the chamber of Othello and Desdemona. He is interrupted by a clown who, for a brief time provides some unexpected low comedy before dismissing the musicians with a gift of money. Then Cassio gives the clown a piece of gold and instructs him to tell Emilia that the lieutenant wishes to talk with her. But it is Iago who next appears with an offer to detain Othello until Cassio can speak to the ensign's wife. As Iago leaves, Cassio praises him as a man who is most "kind and honest" (42).

Emilia greets the lieutenant and expresses her sorrow for his misfortune. From her he learns that Othello, although personally fond of Cassio, will not re-appoint him as second in command because Montano, a man of important family connections, is highly esteemed in Cyprus. Cassio, sure that Iago has advised him soundly, urges Emilia to arrange for him to have "some brief discourse with Desdemona alone" (54-5). Emilia agrees to do so, and the lieutenant fervently expresses his thanks.

It has been argued that this short scene has been included solely to provide some contrasting entertainment for the audience, but it is obvious enough that this and the next scene are transitional ones leading up to the great temptational scene that follows.

Clown. Why, masters, ha' your instruments been at Naples, that they speak i' th' nose thus?
Musician. How, sir, how?
Clown. Are these, I pray, called wind instruments?
Musician. Ay, marry, are they, sir.
Clown. O, thereby hangs a tail.
Musician. Whereby hangs a tale, sir?
Clown. Marry, sir, by many a wind instrument that I know. But, masters, here's money for you: and the general so likes your music that he desires you, for love's sake, to make no more noise with it.
Musician. Well, sir, we will not.
Clown. If you have any music that may not be heard, to't again: but, as they say, to hear music the general does not greatly care.
Musician. We have none such, sir.
Clown. Then put up your pipes in your bag, for I'll away. Go vanish into air, away!
            [*Exit* Musician *with his fellows.*
Cassio. Dost thou hear, my honest friend?
Clown. No, I hear not your honest friend. I hear you.
Cassio. Prithee keep up thy quillets. There's a poor   **24** piece of gold for thee. If the gentlewoman that attends the general's wife be stirring, tell her there's one Cassio entreats her a little favor of speech. Wilt thou do this?
Clown. She is stirring, sir. If she will stir hither, I shall seem to notify unto her.
Cassio. Do, good my friend.   [*Exit* Clown.

Enter IAGO.

                In happy time, Iago.   **31**
Iago. You have not been abed then?
Cassio. Why, no; the day had broke
Before we parted. I have made bold, Iago,
To send in to your wife: my suit to her
Is that she will to virtuous Desdemona
Procure me some access.
Iago.   I'll send her to you presently;
And I'll devise a mean to draw the Moor
Out of the way, that your converse and business
May be more free.
Cassio. I humbly thank you for't.   [*Exit* IAGO.
                I never knew
A Florentine more kind and honest.   **42**

Enter EMILIA.

Emilia. Good morrow, good lieutenant. I am sorry
For your displeasure; but all will sure be well.   **44**
The general and his wife are talking of it,
And she speaks for you stoutly. The Moor replies
That he you hurt is of great fame in Cyprus
And great affinity, and that in wholesome wisdom   **48**
He might not but refuse you; but he protests he
    loves you,   **49**
And needs no other suitor but his likings

24. "quillets": quips.

31. "In happy time": I am glad to see you.

42. "Florentine": even a Florentine.

44. "your displeasure": i.e., that Othello is displeased with you.

48. "affinity": kindred.

49. "might not but": must.

47

To take the safest occasion by the front   51
To bring you in again.
Cassio.   Yet I beseech you,
If you think fit, or that it may be done,
Give me advantage of some brief discourse
With Desdemona alone.
Emilia.   Pray you come in.
I will bestow you where you shall have time
To speak your bosom freely.
Cassio.   I am much bound to you   [*Exeunt.* 57

51. "occasion": opportunity.
    "front": forelock.

57. "your bosom": your inmost thoughts.

Scene two.

(A ROOM IN THE CASTLE)

Enter OTHELLO, IAGO, *and* Gentlemen.

Othello. These letters give, Iago, to the pilot
And by him do my duties to the Senate.   2
That done, I will be walking on the works;   3
Repair there to me.
Iago.   Well, my good lord, I'll do't.
Othello. This fortification, gentlemen, shall we
    see't?
Gentlemen. We'll wait upon your lordship.
                    [*Exeunt.*

2. "do my duties": voice my loyalty.
3. "works": fortifications.

Scene three.

(THE GARDEN OF THE CASTLE)

Enter DESDEMONA, CASSIO, *and* EMILIA.

Desdemona. Be thou assured, good Cassio, I
    will do
All my abilities in thy behalf.
Emilia. Good madam, do. I warrant it grieves my
    husband
As if the cause were his.
Desdemona. O, that's an honest fellow. Do not
    doubt, Cassio,
But I will have my lord and you again
As friendly as you were.
Cassio.   Bounteous madam,
Whatever shall become of Michael Cassio,
He's never anything but your true servant.
Desdemona. I know't; I thank you. You do love
    my lord;
You have known him long; and be you well assured
He shall in strangeness stand no farther off   12
Than in a politic distance.
Cassio.   Ay, but, lady,   13
That policy may either last so long,
Or feed upon such nice and waterish diet,   15

12. "strangeness": aloofness.

13. "Than . . . distance": Than wise considerations dictate.

15. "Or . . . diet": or continued for slight reasons.

ACT III SCENE II

Othello instructs Iago to see to it that certain letters are immediately sent to the Venetian Senate and then to rejoin him. The general leaves to inspect the Cyprian fortifications.

ACT III SCENE III

Desdemona, the well-meaning bride, understandably sure that she can influence her husband, assures Cassio that she will do all she can in his behalf. Emilia adds her wishes that the young lady do so. Her reason is of interest: she is convinced that her husband grieves for Cassio as if he himself had suffered. Now Desdemona is convinced that she can lead Othello to restore the cashiered lieutenant. The latter expresses his gratitude but urges her not to delay since the general, once having appointed a new lieutenant, may forget his love and service. Again Desdemona is most reassuring, stating that it is not in her character to violate a vow of friendship. She will not let the Moor sleep till he accedes to her wishes; she will "talk him out of patience" (23). Thus does the poet-dramatist render probable her persistent but untimely solicitations which follow.

Or breed itself so out of circumstance,
That, I being absent, and my place supplied,
My general will forget my love and service.

Desdemona. Do not doubt that; before Emilia here   19
I give thee warrant of thy place. Assure thee,
If I do vow a friendship, I'll perform it
To the last article. My lord shall never rest;
I'll watch him tame and talk him out of patience;   23
His bed shall seem a school, his board a shrift;   24
I'll intermingle everything he does
With Cassio's suit. Therefore be merry, Cassio,
For thy solicitor shall rather die
Than give thy cause away.

Enter OTHELLO *and* IAGO *at a distance.*

Emilia. Madam, here comes my lord.
Cassio. Madam, I'll take my leave.
Desdemona. Why, stay, and hear me speak.
Cassio. Madam, not now: I am very ill at ease,
Unfit for mine own purposes.
Desdemona. Well, do your discretion. [*Exit* CASSIO.
Iago. Ha! I like not that.
Othello.   What dost thou say?
Iago. Nothing, my lord; or if — I know not what.
Othello. Was not that Cassio parted from my wife?
Iago. Cassio, my lord? No, sure, I cannot think it,
That he would steal away so guilty-like,
Seeing you coming.
Othello.   I do believe 'twas he.
Desdemona. How now, my lord?
I have been talking with a suitor here,
A man that languishes in your displeasure.
Othello. Who is't you mean?
Desdemona. Why, your lieutenant, Cassio. Good my
     lord,
If I have any grace or power to move you,
His present reconciliation take;   47
For if he be not one that truly loves you,
That errs in ignorance, and not in cunning,
I have no judgment in an honest face.
I prithee call him back.
Othello.   Went he hence now?
Desdemona. Yes, faith; so humbled
That he hath left part of his grief with me
To suffer with him. Good love, call him back.
Othello. Not now, sweet Desdemon; some other
     time.
Desdemona. But shall't be shortly?
Othello.   The sooner, sweet, for you.
Desdemona. Shall't be to-night at supper?
Othello.   No, not to-night.

Desdemona. To-morrow dinner then?
Othello.   I shall not dine at home;
I meet the captains at the citadel.
Desdemona. Why then, to-morrow night, or Tues-
     day morn,
On Tuesday noon or night, or Wednesday morn.

When Othello and Iago enter at a distance, Cassio excuses himself, saying that he is too ill at ease to speak with the Moor at this time. And it is at this point that Iago, the brilliant tactician who is ready to make the most of every incident and occasion, begins his attack upon Othello. His approach is a psychological one now, in contrast to that which he employed in discrediting Cassio. But again he is careful to represent himself as the honest, reluctant witness. His "Ha! I like not that" (35) as he observes Cassio leave and then his insistence that he meant nothing seem to be convincingly natural. His words are, of course, filled with innuendo. Note his reply to Othello's question, "Was not that Cassio parted from my wife?" (37). The force of the verb steal and the modifier so guilty-like is obvious. Iago presents himself as a man who cannot believe his eyes. Thus early is the seed of jealousy planted, and one can understand the tone and evidence of perturbation in the Moor's words with Desdemona, who now greets him and who promptly introduces the name of Cassio into the discourse. The pathos of Desdemona's position here and subsequently is that, in her innocence, her timing could hardly have been worse.

There is a tacit comparison between Iago and Cassio in her assurance that the latter "errs in ignorance not in cunning" (49). Othello's questions and statements become short to the point of abruptness. Yet in her plea the young wife ignores her husband's reply: "Not now, sweet Desdemon; some other time" (55)

19. "doubt": fear.

23. "watch him tame": keep after him until he agrees with you.
24. "shrift": confessional.

47. "present": immediate.

I prithee name the time, but let it not
Exceed three days. I' faith, he's penitent;
And yet his trespass, in our common reason
(Save that, they say, the wars must make examples
Out of their best), is not almost a fault   66
T' incur a private check. When shall he come?   67
Tell me, Othello. I wonder in my soul
What you could ask me that I should deny
Or stand so mamm'ring on. What? Michael Cassio,   70
That came a-wooing with you, and so many a time,
When I have spoke of you dispraisingly,
Hath ta'en your part — to have so much to do
To bring him in? By'r Lady, I could do much —   74
   Othello. Prithee no more. Let him come when he
     will!
I will deny thee nothing.
   Desdemona.   Why, this is not a boon;
'Tis as I should entreat you wear your gloves,
Or feed on nourishing dishes, or keep you warm,
Or sue to you to do a peculiar profit
To your own person. Nay, when I have a suit
Wherein I mean to touch your love indeed,
It shall be full of poise and difficult weight,   82
And fearful to be granted.
   Othello.   I will deny thee nothing!
Whereon I do beseech thee grant me this,
To leave me but a little to myself.
   Desdemona. Shall I deny you? No. Farewell, my
     lord.
   Othello. Farewell, my Desdemon: I'll come to thee
     straight.
   Desdemona. Emilia, come. — Be as your fancies
     teach you;
Whate'er you be, I am obedient. [*Exit with* EMILIA.
   Othello. Excellent wretch! Perdition catch my soul 90
But I do love thee! and when I love thee not,
Chaos is come again.
   Iago. My noble lord —
   Othello.   What dost thou say, Iago?
   Iago. Did Michael Cassio, when you wooed my
     lady,
Know of your love?
   Othello. He did, from first to last. Why dost thou
     ask?
   Iago. But for a satisfaction of my thought;
No further harm.
   Othello.   Why of thy thought, Iago?
   Iago. I did not think he had been acquainted with
     her.
   Othello. O, yes, and went between us very oft.
   Iago. Indeed?
   Othello. Indeed? Ay, indeed! Discern'st thou
     aught in that?
Is he not honest?
   Iago.   Honest, my lord?
   Othello.   Honest. Ay, honest.
   Iago. My lord, for aught I know.
   Othello. What dost thou think?

66. "not almost": hardly.

67. "a private check": even a private reproval.

70. "mamm'ring": hesitating.

74. "bring him in": i.e., into your favor.

82. "poise": weight, meaning grave importance.
"difficult weight": hard to estimate.

90. "wretch": (a term of endearment).

Had not Cassio implored her not to delay in her suit? And so she persists, gently reproving her husband for hesitating and reminding him that Cassio had taken his part when he wooed her. Exclaiming that he will deny her nothing, the Moor begs to be left to himself for a time. Perhaps there is an element of prophecy in Desdemona's and Othello's "Farewell" (86-7) as there certainly is in the general's first speech after his wife leaves with Emilia (90-2). In a metaphorical sense, perdition will catch his soul, and chaos will replace order in his life.

Iago resumes his attack with a series of questions, carefully maintaining his pose as a man who is to be trusted. He leads Othello to state that Desdemona had come to know Cassio very well. "Indeed?" he asks (101) with just the right intonation for his purpose, as Othello's repetition of the word tells us. This leads to the question of Cassio's honesty, and it is the villain now who echoes the word and moves to his conclusion: "My lord, for aught I know" (104). When Othello then demands what Iago thinks, it is the verb which is repeated, leading the general to insist that the ensign reveal his thoughts.

OTHELLO

ACT III SCENE III

One sees how skillfully Iago makes use of his public reputation for honesty when Othello concedes that the villain's hesitations frighten him because he knows that they cannot be "tricks of custom" employed by a "false disloyal knave," but come from the ear of one whom "passion can not rule" (118-24). In the lines immediately following notice that the most Iago will say is that he dares "be sworn," that he "thinks" Cassio is honest. Thus does he protect himself and still advance his vicious cause, maneuvering things in such a way that Othello believes the truth must be dragged from him.

As we have seen before, the villain's words can be as true as they are eloquent. He pleads that he is not bound to utter his thoughts and argues that foul things sometimes intrude in places and impure apprehensions may invade "meditations lawful" (133-41). The ensign now has Othello in a position where he becomes only more persistent in his demands that Iago speak his mind. What the villain is doing is to make the Moor believe that honor is at stake. With apparent frankness he acknowledges that he may perhaps be "vicious" in his "guess," states that jealousy often makes him "shape faults that are not," and at the same time refers to the "wisdom" of Othello, implying that the general is not one to be trapped by his emotions (144-56). Filled with what appears to be moral fervor he then proceeds to a peroration on the subject of reputation, which he now describes as priceless. The student, to be sure, will immediately recall his contrasting view on the same subject in lines spoken to the disconsolate Cassio (II.iii.257-64).

Iago.   Think, my lord?
Othello.   Think, my lord?
By heaven, he echoes me,
As if there were some monster in his thought
Too hideous to be shown. Thou dost mean something:
I heard thee say but now, thou lik'st not that,
When Cassio left my wife. What didst not like?
And when I told thee he was of my counsel
In my whole course of wooing, thou cried'st 'Indeed?'
And didst contract and purse thy brow together,
As if thou then hadst shut up in thy brain
Some horrible conceit. If thou dost love me,   115
Show me thy thought.
   Iago. My lord, you know I love you.
Othello.   I think thou dost;
And, for I know thou'rt full of love and honesty
And weigh'st thy words before thou giv'st them breath,
Therefore these stops of thine fright me the more;
For such things in a false disloyal knave
Are tricks of custom; but in a man that's just
They are close dilations, working from the heart   123
That passion cannot rule.
   Iago.   For Michael Cassio,   124
I dare be sworn I think that he is honest.
Othello. I think so too.
   Iago.   Men should be what they seem;
Or those that be not, would they might seem none!   127
Othello. Certain, men should be what they seem.
Iago. Why then, I think Cassio's an honest man.
Othello. Nay, yet there's more in this.
I prithee speak to me as to thy thinkings,
As thou dost ruminate, and give thy worst of thoughts
The worst of words.
   Iago.   Good my lord, pardon me:
Though I am bound to every act of duty,
I am not bound to that all slaves are free to.   135
Utter my thoughts? Why, say they are vile and false,
As where's that palace whereinto foul things
Sometimes intrude not? Who has a breast so pure
But some uncleanly apprehensions
Keep leets and law days, and in session sit   140
With meditations lawful?
   Othello. Thou dost conspire against thy friend, Iago,
If thou but think'st him wronged, and mak'st his ear
A stranger to thy thoughts.
   Iago.   I do beseech you —
Though I perchance am vicious in my guess
(As I confess it is my nature's plague
To spy into abuses, and oft my jealousy   147
Shapes faults that are not), that your wisdom yet
From one that so imperfectly conjects   149
Would take no notice, nor build yourself a trouble
Out of his scattering and unsure observance.   151
It were not for your quiet nor your good,
Nor for my manhood, honesty, or wisdom,
To let you know my thoughts.

115. "conceit": fancy.

123-24. "close . . . rule": secret emotions which are revealed inadvertently.

127. "seem none": i.e., not present themselves as human beings when they are really monsters.

135. "bound . . . free": bound to reveal that which even slaves are permitted to keep to themselves.

140. "leet and law days": sittings of the court.

147. "jealousy": suspicion.

149. "conjects": conjectures.

151. "scattering": random.

OTHELLO

ACT III SCENE III

When Othello again declares that he will know what Iago really thinks, the ensign still holds him off for a time. And then he strikes home with his warning against jealousy, "the green-ey'd monster" which torments those who succumb to it (166-70). Othello's "O misery" tells us that he is already on the rack. If he vigorously denies that he would sink to a state of jealousy, the level of his discourse indicates the great change that has taken place in him. "Exchange me for a goat" (180), with its gross animal image, points to the fact that the noble, valiant Moor is descending on the hierarchical scale of human beings toward the lowest level, the bestial. Prior to this, it was Iago who used such language, notably in his discourse with Roderigo.

Othello states that he will see before he doubts, that he will not become jealous until he has absolute proof that his wife is unfaithful to him. Jealousy, it will be recalled involves not certainty but suspicion in this case. Iago expresses his approval. And why not? He is now in a position to direct Othello, who has come to depend upon him just as Cassio had done earlier. Let the Moor look to his wife; let him observe her well with Cassio — that is the ensign's first counsel. Further to agonize the Moor, as well as to qualify himself as a competent witness, he tells him that he knows the Venetian temperament and habits very well and that the faithless wife is a well-known member of Venetian society. The general, one remembers, had told the Duke and the senators that he knew little of the world except for that pertaining to warfare. Here Iago makes use of Othello's public declaration as he will other declarations of this kind. Thus he follows through by reminding the Moor that Desdemona had deceived her father, who described Othello as a man she had "feared to look on" (I.iii.98) and had insisted that the general used witchcraft in his suit. These are telling lines and Iago is astute enough to pause, begging his superior's forgiveness and attributing his own frankness to his regard to Othello. "I am bound to thee forever," says the Moor, and we know that he indeed has been trapped.

Othello.   What dost thou mean?

Iago. Good name in man and woman, dear my lord,
Is the immediate jewel of their souls.   156
Who steals my purse steals trash; 'tis something, nothing;
'Twas mine, 'tis his, and has been slave to thousands;
But he that filches from me my good name
Robs me of that which not enriches him
And makes me poor indeed.

Othello. By heaven, I'll know thy thoughts!

Iago. You cannot, if my heart were in your hand;
Nor shall not whilst 'tis in my custody.

Othello. Ha!

Iago.   O, beware, my lord, of jealousy!
It is the green-eyed monster, which doth mock   166
The meat it feeds on. That cuckold lives in bliss
Who, certain of his fate, loves not his wronger;
But O, what damned minutes tells he o'er
Who dotes, yet doubts — suspects, yet strongly loves!

Othello. O misery!

Iago. Poor and content is rich, and rich enough;
But riches fineless is as poor as winter   173
To him that ever fears he shall be poor.
Good God the souls of all my tribe defend
From jealousy!

Othello.   Why, why is this?
Think'st thou I'd make a life of jealousy,
To follow still the changes of the moon
With fresh suspicions? No! To be once in doubt
Is once to be resolved. Exchange me for a goat
When I shall turn the business of my soul
To such exsufflicate and blown surmises,   182
Matching thy inference. 'Tis not to make me jealous
To say my wife is fair, feeds well, loves company,
Is free of speech, sings, plays, and dances well;
Where virtue is, these are more virtuous.
Nor from mine own weak merits will I draw
The smallest fear or doubt of her revolt,   188
For she had eyes, and chose me. No, Iago;
I'll see before I doubt; when I doubt, prove;
And on the proof there is no more but this —
Away at once with love or jealousy!

Iago. I am glad of this; for now I shall have reason
To show the love and duty that I bear you
With franker spirit. Therefore, as I am bound,
Receive it from me. I speak not yet of proof.
Look to your wife; observe her well with Cassio;
Wear your eye thus, not jealous nor secure: 198
I would not have your free and noble nature,
Out of self-bounty, be abused. Look to't.   200
I know our country disposition well:
In Venice they do let God see the pranks
They dare not show their husbands; their best conscience
Is not to leave't undone, but keep't unknown.

Othello. Dost thou say so?

Iago. She did deceive her father, marrying you;
And when she seemed to shake and fear your looks,

156. "immediate": closest to the heart.

166. "mock": play with, as does a cat with a mouse.

173. "fineless": unlimited.

182. "exsufflicate . . . surmises": inflated and fly-blown.

188. "revolt": infidelity.

198. "secure": careless.

200. "self-bounty": inherent goodness.

Before the two part, Iago goes to further pains to make Othello believe in him. Cassio, he says, remains his "worthy friend," and the Moor must not exaggerate what has been told him. But the villain knows how well he has succeeded so far. His "I see this hath a little dashed your spirits" (214) is a gross understatement. Othello's short replies ("I will not . . . No, not much moved") give evidence of the extent to which he is now under Iago's influence. When he states that he does "not think but Desdemona's honest" (225), the villain's reply ably serves to inflame the general's suspicions: "Long live she so! and long live you to think so!" (226)

It is Othello now who recalls Brabantio's argument when he makes reference to "nature erring from itself" (227). Iago quickly seizes the chance to paraphrase Brabantio's words stressing the violation of nature. Othello's "Farewell, farewell" (238) is ominous. Iago, still playing a masterful hand, remains just long enough to provide further advice: let Othello content himself with doing no more than keeping a close watch on his young wife; in the meantime, let him think that Iago's "fears" are unfounded. "Fear not my government," says the tormented Moor (256), and we are reminded of his perfect self-command in the preceding action.

She loved them most.
Othello.　　　　　And so she did.
Iago.　　　　　　　　Why, go to then!
She that, so young, could give out such a seeming
To seel her father's eyes up close as oak — 210
He thought 'twas witchcraft — but I am much to
　　blame.
I humbly do beseech you of your pardon
For too much loving you.
Othello.　　　　　I am bound to thee for ever.
Iago. I see this hath a little dashed your spirits.
Othello. Not a jot, not a jot.
Iago.　　　　　　I' faith, I fear it has.
I hope you will consider what is spoke
Comes from my love. But I do see y' are moved
I am to pray you not to strain my speech
To grosser issues nor to larger reach 219
Than to suspicion.
Othello. I will not.
Iago.　　　　　Should you do so, my lord,
My speech should fall into such vile success 222
As my thoughts aim not at. Cassio's my worthy
　　friend —
My lord, I see y' are moved.
Othello.　　　　　No, not much moved:
I do not think but Desdemona's honest. 225
Iago. Long live she so! and long live you to
　　think so!
Othello. And yet, how nature erring from itself —
Iago. Ay, there's the point! as (to be bold with
　　you)
Not to affect many proposed matches
Of her own clime, complexion, and degree,
Whereto we see in all things nature tends —
Foh! one may smell in such a will most rank, 232
Foul disproportion, thoughts unnatural —
But pardon me — I do not in position 234
Distinctly speak of her; though I may fear
Her will, recoiling to her better judgment, 236
May fall to match you with her country forms,
And happily repent.
Othello.　　　　　Farewell, farewell! 238
If more thou dost perceive, let me know more.
Set on thy wife to observe. Leave me, Iago.
Iago. My lord, I take my leave. 　　　　[*Going.*
Othello. Why did I marry? This honest creature
　　doubtless
Sees and knows more, much more, than he unfolds.
Iago. [*returns*] My lord, I would I might entreat
　　your honor
To scan this thing no further: leave it to time.
Although 'tis fit that Cassio have his place,
For sure he fills it up with great ability,
Yet, if you please to hold him off awhile,
You shall by that perceive him and his means.
Note if your lady strain his entertainment 250
With any strong or vehement importunity;
Much will be seen in that. In the mean time
Let me be thought too busy in my fears 253

210. "seel": close.
　　"oak": grain.

219. "To . . . issues": to mean something more than monstrous.

222. "vile success": evil consequences.

225. "honest": chaste.

232. "will": desire, appetite.

234. "position": conviction.

236. "recoiling": reverting.

238. "happily": haply, by chance.

250. "strain his entertainment": urge his recall.

253. "busy": meddlesome.

Next we hear Othello in soliloquy (258-77), and the range of the imagery which he uses underscores the appalling change in his character. The absoluteness of the Moor is indicated in lines 260-3, wherein he states what action he will take if he proves that his wife is unfaithful to him. He then recalls his so-called deficiencies as the husband of a Venetian senator's daughter — his dark skin, his self-admitted inability to talk like a courtier ("Rude am I in my speech" he had told the assembly in the Council Chamber), his age in comparison to that of Desdemona. That it is his pride that has been injured is made clear when he says, "I am abused, and my relief/ Must be to loathe her" (267-8) and especially when he identifies himself with the "great ones" of this world (273-4). To be noted also is the "toad" image (270-1) which conveys the idea of utter loathing. And yet, as Desdemona and Emilia enter, he moves from this to an appeal to heaven (278) when he declares that he will not believe that his wife is false to him.

In his brief discourse with Desdemona, the Moor speaks curtly and faintly as he pleads that he has a headache. When Desdemona offers to bind his head with her handkerchief, he declines the offer on the grounds that the handkerchief is too small. As he pushes it from him, it falls to the floor unnoticed. Both Othello and his wife leave.

Alone, Emilia picks up the handkerchief, and we learn that her "wayward husband" had repeatedly asked her to get it for him. We learn further that it was a gift from Othello to Desdemona, who was told to treasure it. Emilia's motive is an innocent one; she believes that Iago is interested only in the embroidery on the handkerchief. It is notable, however, that twice she uses the word steal when she refers to what Iago wanted her to do (293, 309).

(As worthy cause I have to fear I am)
And hold her free, I do beseech your honor. 255
Othello. Fear not my government. 256
Iago. I once more take my leave.   [*Exit.*
Othello. This fellow's of exceeding honesty,
And knows all qualities, with a learned spirit 259
Of human dealings. If I do prove her haggard, 260
Though that her jesses were my dear heartstrings, 261
I'd whistle her off and let her down the wind 262
To prey at fortune. Haply, for I am black 263
And have not those soft parts of conversation 264
That chamberers have, or for I am declined 265
Into the vale of years — yet that's not much —
She's gone. I am abused, and my relief
Must be to loathe her. O curse of marriage,
That we can call these delicate creatures ours,
And not their appetites! I had rather be a toad
And live upon the vapor of a dungeon
Than keep a corner in the thing I love
For others' uses. Yet 'tis the plague of great ones; 273
Prerogatived are they less than the base. 274
'Tis destiny unshunnable, like death.
Even then this forked plague is fated to us 276
When we do quicken. Look where she comes. 277

Enter DESDEMONA *and* EMILIA.

If she be false, O, then heaven mocks itself!
I'll not believe't.
Desdemona.   How now, my dear Othello?
Your dinner, and the generous islanders 280
By you invited, do attend your presence.
Othello. I am to blame.
Desdemona.   Why do you speak so faintly?
Are you not well?
Othello. I have a pain upon my forehead, here.
Desdemona. Faith, that's with watching; 'twill
    away again. 285
Let me but bind it hard, within this hour
It will be well.
Othello.   Your napkin is too little; 287

[*He pushes the handkerchief from him, and it falls
unnoticed*

Let it alone. Come, I'll go in with you. 288
Desdemona. I am very sorry that you are not well.
    [*Exit with* OTHELLO.
Emilia. I am glad I have found this napkin;
This was her first remembrance from the Moor.
My wayward husband hath a hundred times
Wooed me to steal it; but she so loves the
    token
(For he conjured her she should ever keep it)
That she reserves it evermore about her
To kiss and talk to. I'll have the work ta'en out 296
And give't Iago.
What he will do with it heaven knows, not I;
I nothing but to please his fantasy. 299

255. "hold her free": believe her to be guiltless.
256. "government": self-control.

259. "qualities": natures.
    "learned spirit": of mind informed about.
260. "haggard": a wild hawk.
261. "jesses": thongs for controlling a hawk.
262-63. "whistle . . . fortune": turn her out to shift for herself.
    "for": because.
264. "soft . . . conversation": refined social graces.
265. "chamberers": courtiers and gallants.

273. "great ones": distinguished men."
274. "Prerogatived": privileged.

276. "forked plague": i.e., the cuckold's horns.
277. "quicken": begin to live.

280. "generous": noble.

285. "watching": working late.

287. "napkin": handkerchief.

288. "it": i.e., his forehead.

296. "work . . . out": pattern copied.

299. "fantasy": whim.

OTHELLO

ACT III SCENE III

Iago enters and, after a brief exchange with Emilia, he learns that she has the handkerchief. He snatches it from his wife, refusing to tell why he wants it so badly. Alone on the stage, he then reveals the next step in his plan. He will place the handkerchief in Cassio's lodging and let the former lieutenant find it. Opportunist that he is, he believes that all this will work out to his end. The ensign's mention of Othello tells us that he expects the Moor to find the handkerchief in Cassio's possession. Already prone to be suspicious as a result of Iago's "poison" (325), Othello will draw the conclusion that the ensign wants. The simile used by the villain at the end of this speech, "like mines of sulphur" (329) suggests hell's fire and thus points to the diabolical actions of Iago.

The ensign now sees Othello enter. His speech (330-331) and the longer one by Othello (345-57) mark the climax of this play. Although the climax-deed and the catastrophe are not presented until the last act, Othello is already a fallen man. If the change in the noble Moor seems to have come about too quickly, one should recall how well Shakespeare provided for this by creating an arch-villain who had convinced everybody else that he was a man to be trusted, by having both Iago and Othello recall the chief arguments made by Brabantio before the members of the Council, and by having the Moor dwell upon the disparities between himself and Desdemona. Further, it must be remembered, a dramatist must depend upon economy of means; he does not have the freedom available to the novelist to extend the action and to dwell at great length upon one episode.

We have seen that, especially in soliloquy, Iago usually speaks the truth. Here, he diagnoses Othello's condition. The Moor is a man who will never again find repose. It is a frantic Othello who upbraids the ensign for setting him "on the rack" (335) and who expresses the wish that he had remained blind to his wife's alleged infidelity. His great "farewell" speech that follows emphasizes how much he has lost — he, the premier soldier, whose occupation now is gone! And when Iago appears incredulous, the Moor turns on him with words that make the ensign only too aware of the danger which faces him (359-63, 368-73).

Enter IAGO.

Iago. How now? What do you here alone?
Emilia. Do not you chide; I have a thing for you.
Iago. A thing for me? It is a common thing —
Emilia. Ha?
Iago. To have a foolish wife.
Emilia. O, is that all? What will you give me now
For that same handkerchief?
Iago.   What handkerchief?
Emilia. What handkerchief!
Why, that the Moor first gave to Desdemona;
That which so often you did bid me steal.
Iago. Hast stol'n it from her?
Emilia. No, faith; she let it drop by negligence,
And to th' advantage, I, being here, took't up.   312
Look, here it is.
Iago.   A good wench! Give it me.
Emilia. What will you do with't, that you have been
    so earnest
To have me filch it?
Iago.   Why, what's that to you? [*Snatches it.*
Emilia. If it be not for some purpose of import,   316
Give't me again. Poor lady, she'll run mad
When she shall lack it.
Iago. Be not acknown on't; I have use for it.   319
Go, leave me.   [*Exit* EMILIA.
I will in Cassio's lodging lose this napkin
And let him find it. Trifles light as air
Are to the jealous confirmations strong
As proofs of holy writ. This may do something.
The Moor already changes with my poison:
Dangerous conceits are in their natures poisons,   326
Which at the first are scarce found to distaste,
But with a little act upon the blood
Burn like the mines of sulphur.

Enter OTHELLO.

            I did say so.
Look where he comes! Not poppy nor mandragora,   330
Nor all the drowsy syrups of the world,
Shall ever med'cine thee to that sweet sleep
Which thou owedst yesterday.
Othello.   Ha! ha! false to me?   333
Iago. Why, how now, general? No more of that!
Othello. Avaunt! be gone! Thou hast set me on the
    rack.
I swear 'tis better to be much abused
Than but to know't a little.
Iago.   How now, my lord?
Othello. What sense had I of her stol'n hours of
    lust?
I saw't not, thought it not, it harmed not me;
I slept the next night well, fed well, was free and
    merry;   340
I found not Cassio's kisses on her lips.
He that is robbed, not wanting what is stol'n,   342

312. "to th' advantage": opportunely.

316. "import": importance.

319. "acknown": aware.

326. "conceits": ideas.

330. "mandragora": a soporific to cause sleep.

333. "owedst": hadst.

340. "free": carefree.

342. "wanting": missing.

55

OTHELLO

But Iago knows what must be said to protect himself: another avowal of honesty and concern only for Othello's welfare. The Moor, he says, has taught him a valuable lesson. "I'll love no friend, sith love breeds such offense" (380). The general promptly concedes that Iago should be honest, and the villian knows that, for the time being he is safe. But Othello cannot endure the uncertainty; he must have all doubts removed one way or another. Again Iago diagnoses his condition accurately: "I see, sir, you are eaten up with passion" (391). And in lines notably coarse the villain introduces the subject of what kind of evidence would resolve Othello's doubts. The bestial images, the import of which has already been noticed, are prominent (403-5). When the general first began to succumb to Iago's machinations his own speech began to be colored by comparable images.

Let him not know't, and he's not robbed at all.

Iago. I am sorry to hear this.

Othello. I had been happy if the general camp,
Pioners and all, had tasted her sweet body,   346
So I had nothing known. O, now for ever
Farewell the tranquil mind! farewell content!
Farewell the plumed troop, and the big wars   349
That make ambition virtue! O, farewell!
Farewell the neighing steed and the shrill trump,
The spirit-stirring drum, th' ear-piercing fife,
The royal banner, and all quality,
Pride, pomp, and circumstance of glorious war!   354
And O you mortal engines whose rude throats   355
Th' immortal Jove's dread clamors counterfeit,   356
Farewell! Othello's occupation's gone!

Iago. Is't possible, my lord?

Othello. Villain, be sure thou prove my love a
    whore!
Be sure of it; give me the ocular proof;
Or, by the worth of man's eternal soul,
Thou hadst been better have been born a dog
Than answer my waked wrath!

Iago.   Is't come to this?

Othello. Make me to see't; or at the least so prove it
That the probation bear no hinge nor loop   365
To hang a doubt on — or woe upon thy life!

Iago. My noble lord —

Othello. If thou dost slander her and torture me,
Never pray more; abandon all remorse;
On horror's head horrors accumulate;
Do deeds to make heaven weep, all earth amazed;
For nothing canst thou to damnation add
Greater than that.

Iago.   O grace! O heaven forgive me!
Are you a man? Have you a soul or sense? —
God b' wi' you! take mine office. O wretched fool,
That liv'st to make thine honesty a vice!
A monstrous world! Take note, take note, O world,
To be direct and honest is not safe.
I thank you for this profit; and from hence
I'll love no friend, sith love breeds such offense.

Othello. Nay, stay. Thou shouldst be honest.

Iago. I should be wise; for honesty's a fool
And loses that it works for.

Othello.   By the world,
I think my wife be honest, and think she is not;
I think that thou art just, and think thou art not.
I'll have some proof. Her name, that was as fresh
As Dian's visage, is now begrimed and black
As mine own face. If there be cords, or knives,
Poison, or fire, or suffocating streams,
I'll not endure it. Would I were satisfied!

Iago. I see, sir, you are eaten up with passion:
I do repent me that I put it to you.
You would be satisfied?

Othello.   Would? Nay, I will.   393

Iago. And may; but how? how satisfied, my lord?
Would you, the supervisor, grossly gape on?   395
Behold her topped?

346. "Pioners": Sappers; laborers.

349. "big": impressive.

354. "circumstance": pageantry.

355. "mortal engines": deadly artillery.

356. "counterfeit": imitate.

365. "probation": proof.

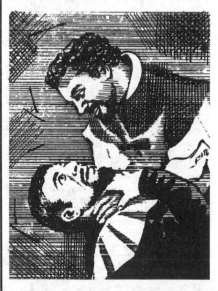

393. "satisfied": fully informed.

395. "supervisor": observer.

56

OTHELLO

ACT III SCENE III

Now, instead of relying upon innuendo, Iago tells a bold lie, claiming that, when he had slept with Cassio recently, the former lieutenant, in words spoken and actions performed in his sleep, made perfectly clear his illicit relations with Desdemona. Othello is beside himself. "O monstrous! monstrous!" he exclaims (427). But the ingenious Iago is quick to remind him that all this was no more than Cassio's dream. Othello thinks otherwise, as Iago knew he would. In his rage he declares that he will tear Desdemona to pieces. And this was the noble Moor who repeatedly had demonstrated such complete command of himself.

Iago, however, will be sure of his man. He does not want to take any risk; he must know that the general will not change his mind. Therefore he makes reference to the handkerchief with its intricate embroidery. Othello immediately recognizes it as the one he had given to Desdemona. Then the ensign tells the Moor that he had seen Cassio wipe his beard with it that very day. The general is enraged to the point where he becomes convinced that all his suspicions are true: "All my fond love thus do I blow to heaven/ 'Tis gone," he exclaims (445-6); and in highly rhetorical lines he dwells upon "black vengeance" and "tyrannous hate" (447-50). Iago urges him to be patient, arguing that he may change his mind. There follows the great Pontic sea simile, the poetic gem of the play, in which Othello compares his "bloody thoughts" to the sea's current which never ebbs but keeps on its course until it reaches its destination, the Propontic and the Hellespont (453-60). It is curious that Alexander Pope approved the omission of this simile in the 1622 Quarto of the play, describing it as "an unnatural excursion" in the drama. So far from being that, it is as highly informing as it is poetical. The simile shows us the Moor stressing his high status, as befits a tragic hero, by identifying himself with one of the larger elements in nature. More important, it makes clear the absoluteness in Othello's character; once he has decided upon which course to take he cannot turn back. And this goes far to make plausible the almost incredible action to follow.

Othello.   Death and damnation! O!

Iago. It were a tedious difficulty, I think,
To bring them to that prospect. Damn them then,
If ever mortal eyes do see them bolster   399
More than their own! What then? How then?
What shall I say? Where's satisfaction?
It is impossible you should see this,
Were they as prime as goats, as hot as monkeys,   403
As salt as wolves in pride, and fools as gross   404
As ignorance made drunk. But yet, I say,
If imputation and strong circumstances
Which lead directly to the door of truth
Will give you satisfaction, you may have't.

Othello. Give me a living reason she's disloyal.

Iago. I do not like the office.
But sith I am entered in this cause so far,
Pricked to't by foolish honesty and love,
I will go on. I lay with Cassio lately,
And being troubled with a raging tooth,
I could not sleep.
There are a kind of men so loose of soul
That in their sleeps will mutter their affairs.
One of this kind is Cassio.
In sleep I heard him say, 'Sweet Desdemona,
Let us be wary, let us hide our loves!'
And then, sir, would he gripe and wring my hand,
Cry 'O sweet creature!' and then kiss me hard,
As if he plucked up kisses by the roots
That grew upon my lips; then laid his leg
Over my thigh, and sighed, and kissed, and then
Cried 'Cursed fate that gave thee to the Moor!'

Othello. O monstrous! monstrous!

Iago.   Nay, this was but his dream.

Othello. But this denoted a foregone conclusion: 428
'Tis a shrewd doubt, though it be but a dream.   429

Iago. And this may help to thicken other proofs
That do demonstrate thinly.

Othello.   I'll tear her all to pieces!

Iago. Nay, but be wise. Yet we see nothing done;
She may be honest yet. Tell me but this—
Have you not sometimes seen a handkerchief
Spotted with strawberries in your wife's hand?

Othello. I gave her such a one; 'twas my first gift.

Iago. I know not that; but such a handkerchief—
I am sure it was your wife's—did I to-day
See Cassio wipe his beard with.

Othello.   If't be that—

Iago. If it be that, or any that was hers,
It speaks against her with the other proofs.

Othello. O, that the slave had forty thousand lives!
One is too poor, too weak for my revenge.
Now do I see 'tis true. Look here, Iago:
All my fond love thus do I blow to heaven.
'Tis gone.
Arise, black vengeance, from the hollow hell!
Yield up, O love, thy crown and hearted throne
To tyrannous hate! Swell, bosom, with thy fraught,   449
For 'tis of aspics' tongues!

Iago.   Yet be content.   450

399. "bolster": lie together.

403. "prime": lustful.

404. "salt": lecherous.

428. "foregone conclusion": earlier experience.

429. "shrewd doubt": strong reason for suspicion.

449. "fraught": burden.

450. "aspics'": asps'.

ACT III SCENE III

Othello solemnly vows to execute "a capable and wide revenge" and kneels (459). His use of the words heaven, reverence, and sacred suggest that he already sees himself as one executing public justice, as the scourge of evil, rather than as one seeking personal revenge. Bidding the Moor not to rise yet, Iago also kneels and dedicates himself to "wronged Othello's service" (467). As both rise, the general greets the villain's "love" and states that he will put the ensign to test at once: let him see to it that Cassio is slain within three days. "My friend is dead," Iago replies: "'Tis done at your request." There is, of course, irony in his use of the the word friend here, and the last clause shows how well Iago continues to protect himself. When the ensign urges the general to spare the life of Desdemona, Othello can only curse her as a "lewd minx" and ask the villain to provide him "some swift means of death for her" (475-8). So completely entraoped is the Moor that he appoints Iago, the embodiment of evil, his lieutenant. That he is indeed a lost soul is apparent from Iago's final line in this scene: "I am your own for ever."

ACT III SCENE IV

This and the first two scenes in Act IV are to be justified primarily on the grounds that they provide us an opportunity to observe the fallen Othello prior to the climax-deed, after which there is not cause to believe that he may yet be saved. In other words, the results of Iago's conquest of the Moor are clearly presented at some length as the action moves toward the catastrophe.

The scene opens with some twenty lines of broad comedy provided by the Clown and intended, no doubt, to relieve the great tension of the previous scene. It really amuses the reader or spectator very little. In his routine the Clown depends largely upon word play involving the verb lie.

Othello. O, blood, blood, blood!

Iago. Patience, I say. Your mind perhaps may change.

Othello. Never, Iago. Like to the Pontic sea,   453
Whose icy current and compulsive course
Ne'er feels retiring ebb, but keeps due on
To the Propontic and the Hellespont,
Even so my bloody thoughts, with violent pace,
Shall ne'er look back, ne'er ebb to humble love,
Till that a capable and wide revenge   459
Swallow them up. [*He kneels.*] Now, by yond marble heaven,
In the due reverence of a sacred vow
I here engage my words.

Iago.   Do not rise. [*Iago kneels.*
Witness, you ever-burning lights above,
You elements that clip us round about,   464
Witness that here Iago doth give up
The execution of his wit, hands, heart   466
To wronged Othello's service! Let him command,
And to obey shall be in me remorse,   468
What bloody business ever.   [*They rise.*

Othello.   I greet thy love,
Not with vain thanks but with acceptance bounteous,
And will upon the instant put thee to't.
Within these three days let me hear thee say
That Cassio's not alive.

Iago. My friend is dead; 'tis done at your request.
But let her live.

Othello.   Damn her, lewd minx! O, damn her!
Come, go with me apart. I will withdraw
To furnish me with some swift means of death
For the fair devil. Now art thou my lieutenant.

Iago. I am your own for ever.   [*Exeunt.*

Scene four.

(BEFORE THE CASTLE)

Enter DESDEMONA, EMILIA, *and* Clown.

Desdemona. Do you know, sirrah, where Lieutenant Cassio lies?

Clown. I dare not say he lies anywhere.   3

Desdemona. Why, man?

Clown. He's a soldier, and for me to say a soldier lies is stabbing.

Desdemona. Go to. Where lodges he?

Clown. To tell you where he lodges is to tell you where I lie.

Desdemona. Can anything be made of this?

Clown. I know not where he lodges; and for me to devise a lodging, and say he lies here or he lies there, were to lie in mine own throat.

Desdemona. Can you enquire him out, and be edified by report?

453. "Pontic Sea": Black Sea.

459. "capable": comprehensive.

464. "clip": embrace.

466. "execution": action.
"wit": mind.

468. "remorse": obligation involving pity.

3. "lies": lodges, lives.

We find Desdemona anxious to see Cassio, whom she still addresses as "Lieutenant," and she orders the Clown to find him and tell him that she has already begun her suit to Othello on his behalf. When the Clown leaves she asks Emilia where she could have lost her handkerchief. Emilia tells an outright lie: "I know not, madam" (25). Nor does she correct herself when Desdemona tells her how much the handkerchief is valued. This, and the fact that she still remains silent when Othello harasses his wife (37 ff.) tells greatly against Emilia at this stage of the action. One might reasonably conclude that she is indeed a fit wife for the vicious Iago. However, we must withold our judgment for a time.

Desdemona finds comfort in the belief that the Moor is not one to become jealous if he were to learn about the handkerchief — another example of dramatic irony, coming as this does after the great temptation scene. The way having been prepared so well for his entrance, Othello then appears and, despite his attempts to appear normal, immediately reveals himself as passion's slave. Poisoned by Iago, he now tends to think and to speak much like his newly appointed lieutenant. Thus he says, "Give me your hand. This hand is moist, my lady . . . Hot, hot, and moist" (37-40) and goes on to suggest that Desdemona is unchaste. The palm, if hot and moist, was believed to be an indication of strong sexual desires. Hers, says the Moor, is a "liberal hand," that is, one that she gives too freely to others. The tragic irony lies in the fact that Othello, in a sense, has taken Iago's place as the evil thinker who preys upon the innocent.

Desdemona understandably is puzzled: she cannot speak of such matters. Changing the subject, she reminds Othello of his promise to deny her nothing and tells her husband that, at her bidding, Cassio is coming to speak with him. How unfortunately bad her timing is needs hardly to be pointed out. The Moor will not be put aside. He complains of a cold and asks his wife to lend him her handkerchief. When she hands him one that is not the handkerchief he is concerned about, he reproves her:

Clown. I will catechize the world for him; that is, make questions, and by them answer.

Desdemona. Seek him, bid him come hither. Tell him I have moved my lord on his behalf and hope all will be well.

Clown. To do this is within the compass of man's wit, and therefore I'll attempt the doing of it. [*Exit.*

Desdemona. Where should I lose that handerchief, Emilia?

Emilia. I know not, madam.

Desdemona. Believe me, I had rather have lost my purse
Full of crusadoes; and but my noble Moor   27
Is true of mind, and made of no such baseness
As jealous creatures are, it were enough
To put him to ill thinking.

Emilia.   Is he not jealous?

Desdemona. Who? he? I think the sun where he was born
Drew all such humors from him.

Enter OTHELLO.

Emilia.   Look where he comes.   32

Desdemona. I will not leave him now till Cassio
Be called to him. — How is't with you, my lord?

Othello. Well, my good lady. [*aside*] O, hardness to dissemble! —
How do you, Desdemona?

Desdemona.   Well, my good lord.

Othello. Give me your hand. This hand is moist, my lady.

Desdemona. It yet hath felt no age nor known no sorrow.

Othello. This argues fruitfulness and liberal heart.
Hot, hot, and moist. This hand of yours requires
A sequester from liberty, fasting and prayer,   41
Much castigation, exercise devout;
For here's a young and sweating devil here
That commonly rebels. 'Tis a good hand,
A frank one.

Desdemona.   You may, indeed, say so;
For 'twas that hand that gave away my heart.

Othello. A liberal hand! The hearts of old gave hands;
But our new heraldry is hands, not hearts.   48

Desdemona. I cannot speak of this. Come now, your promise!

Othello. What promise, chuck?

Desdemona. I have sent to bid Cassio come speak with you.

Othello. I have a salt and sorry rheum offends me.   52
Lend me thy handkerchief.

Desdemona.   Here, my lord.

Othello. That which I gave you.

Desdemona.   I have it not about me.

Othello. Not?

Desdemona. No, faith, my lord.

Othello.   That is a fault.
That handkerchief

27. "crusadoes": Portuguese gold coins.

32. "humors": inclinations.

41. "sequester": separation.

48. "heraldry": heraldic symbolism.

52. "salt . . . rheum": distressing head cold.

OTHELLO

ACT III SCENE IV

"That is a fault" (55). It is then that he tells her of its magical properties, that of insuring tranquility and faith in both receiver and giver (56-67). Significant is his report that to lose the handkerchief, according to his mother, was to invite disaster. Now indeed Desdemona is distressed, and she expresses the wish that she had never seen it. Othello seizes upon this statement almost to overwhelm her with questions, while the innocent young wife keeps asking him to see Cassio or at least to talk of him with her. At one point the Moor says: "My mind misgives" (89). This has been called sometimes an illogical retreat to mere suspicion — illogical in view of Othello's certainty as indicated in the previous scene. More reasonably it may be argued that Othello, in the presence of his attractive wife, momentarily expresses the hope that he may be wrong in his judgment of her. His demand for the handkerchief now becomes a refrain, and when Desdemona still persists in her suit for Cassio the Moor can only exclaim "Zounds!" and leave her.

In a brief exchange between Emilia and Desdemona, the former asks if Othello is not jealous. The latter replies that she never before had seen him behave in such a manner. The young wife expresses her belief that the handkerchief must possess some wondrous quality. Emilia, who now emerges as the worldly matron, replies that one does not learn about a man in a short time and that all men behave egocentrically toward women. She is, of course, basing her judgment on her relations with Iago. But more than this, her reply implies that everyone must be put to the test before a sound conclusion can be made concerning him. Othello has experienced such a test. That it was a most difficult one is only consistent with his status as protagonist in the play.

Did an Egyptian to my mother give.	57
She was a charmer, and could almost read	58
The thoughts of people. She told her, while she kept it,	
'Twould make her amiable and subdue my father	60
Entirely to her love; but if she lost it	
Or made a gift of it, my father's eye	
Should hold her loathly, and his spirits should hunt	
After new fancies. She, dying, gave it me,	
And bid me, when my fate would have me wive,	
To give it her. I did so; and take heed on't;	
Make it a darling like your precious eye.	
To lose't or give't away were such perdition	68
As nothing else could match.	

Desdemona.   Is't possible?

Othello. 'Tis true. There's magic in the web of it.
A sibyl that had numbered in the world
The sun to course two hundred compasses,   72
In her prophetic fury sewed the work;
The worms were hallowed that did breed the silk;
And it was dyed in mummy which the skillful   75
Conserved of maidens' hearts.

Desdemona.   I' faith? Is't true?   76

Othello. Most veritable. Therefore look to't well.

Desdemona. Then would to God that I had never
    seen't!

Othello. Ha! Wherefore?

Desdemona. Why do you speak so startingly and
    rash?

Othello. Is't lost? Is't gone? Speak, is it out o' th'
    way?

Desdemona. Heaven bless us!

Othello. Say you?

Desdemona. It is not lost. But what an if it were?

Othello. How?

Desdemona. I say it is not lost.

Othello.   Fetch't, let me see't!

Desdemona. Why, so I can, sir; but I will not now.
This is a trick to put me from my suit:
Pray you let Cassio be received again.

Othello. Fetch me the handkerchief! My mind
    misgives.

Desdemona. Come, come!
You'll never meet a more sufficient man.

Othello. The handkerchief!

Desdemona.   I pray talk me of Cassio.

Othello. The handkerchief!

Desdemona.   A man that all his time
Hath founded his good fortunes on your love,
Shared dangers with you —

Othello. The handkerchief!

Desdemona. I'faith, you are to blame.

Othello. Zounds!   [*Exit.*

Emilia. Is not this man jealous?

Desdemona. I ne'er saw this before.
Sure there's some wonder in this handkerchief;
I am most unhappy in the loss of it.

Emilia. 'Tis not a year or two shows us a man.
They are all but stomachs, and we all but food;

57. "Egyptian": Gypsy.	
58. "charmer": sorcerer.	
60. "amiable": lovable.	
68. "perdition": disaster.	
72. "compasses": annual rounds.	
75. "mummy": embalming fluid.	
76. "conserved": prepared.	

Iago and Cassio enter, the villain still urging Cassio to continue to importune Desdemona. When the former lieutenant immediately follows his advice, Desdemona bewails the fact that, because of her husband's strange behavior she has not been able to move him yet. Cassio, she concludes, must be patient; she will do all she can for him. Iago appears amazed at this report. Can Othello be angry — the man whom he had seen under such perfect control on the battlefield? The ensign leaves to find his superior.

Desdemona is sure that something relating to Othello's public responsibilities or "some unhatched practice" — some plot — has disturbed her husband seriously. When Emilia expresses her fervent wish that Othello has not become jealous, the distressed wife states that she never gave him reason to become so. Again it is the worldly Emilia who replies that "jealous souls will not be answered so" (160). Desdemona voices a brief prayer that the "monster" jealousy will never prey upon her husband, to which Emilia says "amen." Instructing Cassio to remain in the vicinity, Desdemona leaves with Emilia to find the Moor. The essential thing in this dialogue to be remembered between Desdemona and Emilia is that the poet-dramatist succeeds in providing a strong element of suspense. At this point we well hope that Iago will be revealed as the engineer of the plot to ruin Othello.

They eat us hungrily, and when they are full,
They belch us.

Enter IAGO *and* CASSIO.

      Look you — Cassio and my husband!
Iago. There is no other way; 'tis she must do 't.
And lo the happiness! Go and importune her.   109
  Desdemona. How now, good Cassio? What's the
    news with you?
  Cassio. Madam, my former suit. I do beseech you
That by your virtuous means I may again   112
Exist, and be a member of his love
Whom I with all the office of my heart
Entirely honor. I would not be delayed.
If my offense be of such mortal kind
That neither service past, nor present sorrows,
Nor purposed merit in futurity,
Can ransom me into his love again,
But to know so must be my benefit.
So shall I clothe me in a forced content,
And shut myself up in some other course,   122
To fortune's alms.
  Desdemona.   Alas, thrice-gentle Cassio!
My advocation is not now in tune.   124
My lord is not my lord; nor should I know him,
Were he in favor as in humor altered.   126
So help me every spirit sanctified
As I have spoken for you all my best
And stood within the blank of his displeasure   129
For my free speech! You must awhile be patient.
What I can do I will; and more I will
Than for myself I dare. Let that suffice you.
  Iago. Is my lord angry?
  Emilia.   He went hence but now,
And certainly in strange unquietness.
  Iago. Can he be angry? I have seen the cannon
When it hath blown his ranks into the air
And, like the devil, from his very arm
Puffed his own brother — and can he be angry?
Something of moment then. I will go meet him.
There's matter in 't indeed if he be angry.
  Desdemona. I prithee do so.   [*Exit* IAGO.
          Something sure of state, 141
Either from Venice or some unhatched practice   142
Made demonstrable here in Cyprus to him,
Hath puddled his clear spirit; and in such cases   144
Men's natures wrangle with inferior things,
Though great ones are their object. 'Tis even so;
For let our finger ache, and it endues   147
Our other, healthful members even to that sense
Of pain. Nay, we must think men are not gods,
Nor of them look for such observancy
As fits the bridal. Beshrew me much, Emilia,
I was, unhandsome warrior as I am,   152
Arraigning his unkindness with my soul;   153
But now I find I had suborned the witness,
And he's indicted falsely.
  Emilia. Pray heaven it be state matters, as you
    think,
And no conception nor no jealous toy   157

109. "happiness": luck.

112. "virtuous": effective.

122. "shut . . . in": confine myself to.

124. "advocation": advocacy.

126. "favor": appearance.

129. "blank": target, bull's eye.

141. "state": public affairs.
142. "unhatched practice": budding plot.

144. "puddled": muddied.

147. "endues": brings.

152. "unhandsome warrior": unskilled soldier.
153. "arraigning . . . soul": indicting her unkindness before the bar of my soul.

157. "toy": fancy.

After their departure, Bianca, a Cyprian courtesan, joins Cassio, who addresses her in affectionate terms. She scolds him for having kept away from her lodgings for a full week. (We have here an example of the "long time" discussed in the Introduction). Cassio asks to be forgiven, explaining that he has been a troubled man. He gives Bianca Desdemona's handkerchief and instructs her to take out the strawberry pattern thereon. The courtesan suspects that it is "some token from a newer friend" who has replaced her in Cassio's affections. Cassio scoffs and mildly upbraids her for becoming jealous without cause. Bianca persists in her demand that he tell her whose handkerchief it is. But Cassio can only explain that he does not know, that he had found it in his chamber and, admiring the workmanship, had planned to have it copied. It will be noted that the theme of jealousy, if at a far different level, is maintained in this action. Assuring her that he loves her, Cassio urges Bianca to leave him for a time since he awaits the arrival of Othello.

Concerning you.

Desdemona. Alas the day! I never gave him cause.

Emilia. But jealous souls will not be answered so;
They are not ever jealous for the cause,
But jealous for they are jealous. 'Tis a monster
Begot upon itself, born on itself.

Desdemona. Heaven keep that monster from
Othello's mind!

Emilia. Lady, amen.

Desdemona. I will go seek him. Cassio, walk here
about:
If I do find him, I'll move your suit
And seek to effect it to my uttermost.

Cassio. I humbly thank your ladyship.

[*Exeunt* DESDEMONA *and* EMILIA.

Enter BIANCA.

Bianca. Save you, friend Cassio!

Cassio. What make you from home?
How is it with you, my most fair Bianca?
I' faith, sweet love, I was coming to your house.

Bianca. And I was going to your lodging, Cassio.
What, keep a week away? seven days and nights?
Eightscore eight hours? and lovers' absent hours,
More tedious than the dial eightscore times?   176
O weary reck'ning!

Cassio. Pardon me, Bianca:
I have this while with leaden thoughts been pressed;
But I shall in a more continuate time   179
Strike off this score of absence. Sweet Bianca.

[*Gives her* DESDEMONA'S *handkerchief.*

Take me this work out.

Bianca. O Cassio, whence came this?   181
This is some token from a newer friend.
To the felt absence now I feel a cause.
Is't come to this? Well, well.

Cassio. Go to, woman!
Throw your vile guesses in the devil's teeth,
From whence you have them. You are jealous now
That this is from some mistress, some remembrance.
No, by my faith, Bianca.

Bianca. Why, whose is it?

Cassio. I know not, sweet; I found it in my chamber.
I like the work well; ere it be demanded,
As like enough it will, I'd have it copied.
Take it and do't, and leave me for this time.

Bianca. Leave you? Wherefore?

Cassio. I do attend here on the general
And think it no addition, nor my wish,   195
To have him see me womaned.

Bianca. Why, I pray you?

Cassio. Not that I love you not.

Bianca. But that you do not love me!
I pray you bring me on the way a little,
And say if I shall see you soon at night.

Cassio. 'Tis but a little way that I can bring you,
For I attend here; but I'll see you soon.

Bianca. 'Tis very good. I must be circumstanced.   202

[*Exeunt.*

176. "dial": clock.

179. "continuate": uninterrupted.

181. "Take . . . out": copy this embroidery for me.

195. "addition": credit.

202. "circumstanced": reconciled.

In the first part of this scene Iago, ostensibly seeking to comfort Othello, continues to torment the general with his lascivious discourse on the subject of infidelity. When the villain provides specific details, Othello states: "The devil their virtue tempts, and they tempt heaven" (8). This line is weighty with import, for the Moor's virtue has been tempted by a kind of devil in human form and thus tempts heaven. How successful Iago has been and continues to be is only too clear. Othello appears here near the lowest rung on the hierarchical ladder of humanity, completely in the ensign's power. Easily he is convinced that Cassio has even boasted of his conquest of Desdemona, and the very thought of such depravity makes him become incoherent and to fall into a swoon, which, if one chooses to find symbolism in the action, represents his own descent from a state of innocence. "Work on my medicine," says Iago, and he refers to the Moor as "a credulous fool" (46) before he attempts to arouse the general.

ACT FOUR, scene one.

(THE SAME)

Enter OTHELLO *and* IAGO.

Iago. Will you think so?
Othello.   Think so, Iago?
Iago.   What,
To kiss in private?
Othello.   An unauthorized kiss.
Iago. Or to be naked with her friend in bed
An hour or more, not meaning any harm?
Othello. Naked in bed, Iago, and not mean harm?
It is hypocrisy against the devil.   6
They that mean virtuously, and yet do so,
The devil their virtue tempts, and they tempt heaven.
Iago. So they do nothing, 'tis a venial slip.
But if I give my wife a handkerchief —
Othello. What then?
Iago. Why, then 'tis hers, my lord; and being hers,
She may, I think, bestow't on any man.
Othello. She is protectress of her honor too;
May she give that?
Iago. Her honor is an essence that's not seen;
They have it very oft that have it not.
But for the handkerchief —
Othello. By heaven, I would most gladly have forgot it!
Thou said'st — O, it comes o'er my memory
As doth the raven o'er the infected house,   21
Boding to all! — he had my handkerchief.
Iago. Ay, what of that?
Othello.   That's not so good now.
Iago.   What
If I had said I had seen him do you wrong?
Or heard him say — as knaves be such abroad
Who having, by their own importunate suit,
Or voluntary dotage of some mistress,
Convinced or supplied them, cannot choose   28
But they must blab —
Othello.   Hath he said anything?
Iago. He hath, my lord; but be you well assured,
No more than he'll unswear.
Othello.   What hath he said?
Iago. Faith, that he did — I know not what he did.
Othello. What? what?
Iago. Lie —
Othello. With her?
Iago.   With her, on her; what you will.
Othello. Lie with her? lie on her? — We say lie on
her when they belie her. — Lie with her! Zounds,
that's fulsome. — Handkerchief — confessions —
handkerchief! — To confess, and be hanged for his
labor — first to be hanged, and then to confess! I
tremble at it. Nature would not invest herself in such   40
shadowing passion without some instruction. It is   41

63

6. "hypocrisy . . . devil": feigned sin instead of pretended virtue.

21. "infected": plague-stricken.

28. "convinced or supplied": overcame or gratified.

40-1. "invest . . . instruction": i.e., create such imaginations without your tutoring.

OTHELLO

Cassio enters and is told that this is the second fit of epilepsy that Othello has had and that he must have quiet or else he will foam at the mouth. Before Cassio leaves, the villain tells him that he wants very much to speak with him.

When Othello does revive, he is given no respite from his agony as Iago continues to poison his mind. Sardonically the newly appointed lieutenant argues that, since the Moor knows his wife is unfaithful, his lot is better than that of the "millions" who are so victimized without their knowing it. Othello can only praise the wisdom of Iago and continue to be easily led by the nose. As we follow the action in this scene, it is apparent that nowhere else in Shakespeare does a tragic hero come so close to being utterly contemptible. He is placed in the ignominious position of hiding and spying upon the man he believes to be his rival for Desdemona's affections.

not words that shakes me thus. — Pish! Noses, ears, and lips? Is't possible? — Confess? — Handkerchief? — O devil!   [*Falls in a trance.*

Iago. Work on,
My med'cine, work! Thus credulous fools are caught,
And many worthy and chaste dames even thus,
All guiltless, meet reproach. — What, ho! my lord!
My lord, I say! Othello!

        Enter CASSIO.
          How now, Cassio?

Cassio. What's the matter?

Iago. My lord is fall'n into an epilepsy.
This is his second fit; he had one yesterday.

Cassio. Rub him about the temples.

Iago.   No, forbear.
The lethargy must have his quiet course.
If not, he foams at mouth, and by and by   55
Breaks out to savage madness. Look, he stirs.
Do you withdraw yourself a little while.
He will recover straight. When he is gone,
I would on great occasion speak with you.

               [*Exit* CASSIO.
How is it, general? Have you not hurt your head?

Othello. Dost thou mock me?

Iago.   I mock you? No, by heaven.
Would you would bear your fortune like a man!

Othello. A horned man's a monster and a beast.   63

Iago. There's many a beast then in a populous city,
And many a civil monster.   65

Othello. Did he confess it?

Iago.   Good sir, be a man.
Think every bearded fellow that's but yoked
May draw with you. There's millions now alive
That nightly lie in those unproper beds   69
Which they dare swear peculiar: your case is better. 70
O, 'tis the spite of hell, the fiend's arch-mock,
To lip a wanton in a secure couch,   72
And to suppose her chaste! No, let me know;
And knowing what I am, I know what she shall be.

Othello. O, thou art wise! 'Tis certain.

Iago.   Stand you awhile apart;
Confine yourself but in a patient list.   76
Whilst you were here, o'erwhelmed with your grief —
A passion most unsuiting such a man —
Cassio came hither. I shifted him away
And laid good 'scuse upon your ecstasy: 80
Bade him anon return, and here speak with me;
The which he promised. Do but encave yourself 82
And mark the fleers, the gibes, and notable scorns
That dwell in every region of his face;
For I will make him tell the tale anew —
Where, how, how oft, how long ago, and when
He hath, and is again to cope your wife.   87
I say, but mark his gesture. Marry, patience!
Or I shall say you are all in all in spleen,   89
And nothing of a man.

Othello.   Dost thou hear, Iago?

55. "by and by": straightway.

63. "A horned man's": a cuckold's.

65. "civil": polite.

69. "unproper": not exclusively their own.
70. "peculiar": their own.

72. "secure": believed safe from others.

76. "a patient list": the limits of patience.

80. "ecstasy": trance.

82. "encave": hide.

87. "cope": meet.

89. "spleen": anger.

OTHELLO

ACT IV SCENE I

In soliloquy Iago again tells us what his next step will be: to question Cassio regarding the courtesan Bianca while Othello overhears the two. And that is exactly what he does, once Cassio returns. To be sure the name of Bianca is not mentioned, and the deluded Othello, hidden at one side of the stage, can only speak lines which emphasize the torment he suffers as Cassio speaks freely of his relations with the courtesan.

I will be found most cunning in my patience;
But — dost thou hear? — most bloody.
Iago.   That's not amiss;
But yet keep time in all. Will you withdraw?
[OTHELLO *retires.*
Now will I question Cassio of Bianca,
A huswife that by selling her desires   95
Buys herself bread and clothes. It is a creature
That dotes on Cassio, as 'tis the strumpet's plague
To beguile many and be beguiled by one.
He, when he hears of her, cannot refrain
From the excess of laughter. Here he comes.

Enter CASSIO.

As he shall smile, Othello shall go mad;
And his unbookish jealousy must conster   102
Poor Cassio's smiles, gestures, and light behavior
Quite in the wrong. How do you now, lieutenant?
Cassio. The worser that you give me the addition 105
Whose want even kills me.
Iago. Ply Desdemona well, and you are sure on't.
Now, if this suit lay in Bianca's power,
How quickly should you speed!
Cassio.   Alas, poor caitiff!   109
Othello. Look how he laughs already!
Iago. I never knew a woman love man so.
Cassio. Alas, poor rogue! I think, i' faith, she loves
    me.
Othello. Now he denies it faintly, and laughs it out.
Iago. Do you hear, Cassio?
Othello.   Now he importunes him
To tell it o'er. Go to! Well said, well said!
Iago. She gives it out that you shall marry her.
Do you intend it?
Cassio. Ha, ha, ha!
Othello. Do you triumph, Roman? Do you triumph?
Cassio. I marry her? What, a customer? Prithee 120
bear some charity to my wit; do not think it so un-
wholesome. Ha, ha, ha!
Othello. So, so, so, so! They laugh that win!
Iago. Faith, the cry goes that you shall marry her.
Cassio. Prithee say true.
Iago. I am a very villain else.
Othello. Have you scored me? Well.   127
Cassio. This is the monkey's own giving out. She is
persuaded I will marry her out of her own love and
flattery, not out of my promise.
Othello. Iago beckons me; now he begins the story. 131
Cassio. She was here even now; she haunts me in
every place. I was t' other day talking on the sea
bank with certain Venetians, and thither comes the
bauble, and, by this hand, she falls me thus about 135
my neck —
Othello. Crying 'O dear Cassio!' as it were. His
gesture imports it.
Cassio. So hangs, and lolls, and weeps upon me;
so hales and pulls me! Ha, ha, ha!   140

95. "huswife": hussy.

102. "unbookish": uninformed.
    "conster": construe.

105. "addition": title.

109. "caitiff": wretch.

120. "customer": prostitute.

127. "scored": branded.

131. "beckons": signals.

135. "bauble": toy.

140. "hales": hauls.

Bianca, we learn, hopes to marry him, but he laughing denies that he will oblige her. Then the woman herself enters. Rather curiously Othello does not consider the fact that both Cassio and Iago had been talking about her rather than Desdemona before her entrance, for he hears her voice and her very name. What now appalls him is to learn that the courtesan has his wife's handkerchief, which he takes to be a gift from Cassio. When Bianca leaves, Cassio follows Iago's advice to follow her in order to quiet her down.

As he comes forward, Othello's first question speaks volumes: "How shall I murder him, Iago?" (173) He is determined that neither Cassio nor Desdemona shall live. He would have his wife "rot"; he would "hang her"; he "will chop her into messes"; he will "poison" her. No punishment could be too severe for one who had so sullied Othello's reputation and injured his pride. Iago feeds him lines appropriate to the villain's purpose. Particularly he wants the Moor to execute revenge promptly, for he knows that he remains in a dangerous position.

Othello. Now he tells how she plucked him to my chamber. O, I see that nose of yours, but not that dog I shall throw't to.

Cassio. Well, I must leave her company.

Enter BIANCA.

Iago. Before me! Look where she comes.

Cassio. 'Tis such another fitchew! marry, a perfumed one. What do you mean by this haunting of me? 146

Bianca. Let the devil and his dam haunt you! What did you mean by that same handkerchief you gave me even now? I was a fine fool to take it. I must take out the whole work? A likely piece of work that you should find it in your chamber and know not who left it there! This is some minx's token, and I must take out the work? There! Give it your hobby-horse. Wheresoever you had it, I'll take out no work on't. 156

Cassio. How now, my sweet Bianca? How now? how now?

Othello. By heaven, that should be my handkerchief!

Bianca. An you'll come to supper to-night, you may; an you will not, come when you are next prepared for. [*Exit.*

Iago. After her, after her!

Cassio. Faith, I must; she'll rail i' th' street else.

Iago. Will you sup there?

Cassio. Yes, I intend so.

Iago. Well, I may chance to see you; for I would very fain speak with you.

Cassio. Prithee come. Will you?

Iago. Go to! say no more. [*Exit,* CASSIO.

Othello. (*comes forward*) How shall I murder him, Iago?

Iago. Did you perceive how he laughed at his vice?

Othello. O Iago!

Iago. And did you see the handkerchief?

Othello. Was that mine?

Iago. Yours, by this hand! And to see how he prizes the foolish woman your wife! She gave it him, and he hath giv'n it his whore.

Othello. I would have him nine years a-killing! — A fine woman! a fair woman! a sweet woman!

Iago. Nay, you must forget that.

Othello. Ay, let her rot, and perish, and be damned to-night; for she shall not live. No, my heart is turned to stone; I strike it, and it hurts my hand. O, the world hath not a sweeter creature! She might lie by an emperor's side and command him tasks.

Iago. Nay, that's not your way.

Othello. Hang her! I do but say what she is. So delicate with her needle! an admirable musician! O, she will sing the savageness out of a bear! Of so high and plenteous wit and invention —

Iago. She's the worse for all this.

Othello. O, a thousand thousand times! And then, of so gentle a condition! 196

Iago. Ay, too gentle.

146. "fitchew": polecat (meaning whore).

156. "hobby-horse": harlot.

196. "condition": disposition.

OTHELLO

ACT IV SCENE I

When Othello says "I would have him nine years a-killing!" the newly appointed lieutenant is quick to say, "Nay, you must forget that" (183). A bit later he recommends the correct way to dispose of a faithless wife: "Strangle her in her bed, even the bed she contaminated" (210-11), an act the "justice" of which appeals to the Moor.

If indeed Othello now appears so bestial, so devoid of reason, Shakespeare nevertheless depicts him as a man who can still invite some sympathy. We never forget that his adversary emerged as an arch-fiend, that the temptation was no ordinary one. Immediately important in this connection, however, is a key line spoken by the general: "But yet the pity of it, Iago! O Iago, the pity of it, Iago!" (198).

Enter Lodovico, Desdemona, and Attendants. We have reached the so-called "brothel" part of this scene, wherein words and actions would seem incredible if Shakespeare had not prepared so well.

Lodovico, a kinsman of the aristocratic Brabantio, has arrived as emissary from the Venetian Senate. His cordial welcome is at once inadvertently ominous and ironic: "God save you, worthy general" (219). For so fallen is the Moor that no mortal can save him; and he is no longer "worthy" as he was through Act III, scene ii.

Othello recovers himself sufficiently to take care of the immediate amenities. While he reads the communication from Venice, Lodovico learns from Iago that Cassio is in disgrace. Desdemona describes the division between her husband and the former lieutenant as "A most unhappy one" and speaks of her high regard for Cassio (233). The mere mention of that name is enough to inflame the Moor. Not only does he publicly berate her as a dissembling devil, but he goes so far as to strike her and finally to order her to leave:

Othello. Nay, that's certain. But yet the pity of it, Iago! O Iago, the pity of it, Iago!

Iago. If you are so fond over her iniquity, give her patent to offend; for if it touch not you, it comes near nobody. 201

Othello. I will chop her into messes! Cuckold me! 203

Iago. O, 'tis foul in her.

Othello. With mine officer!

Iago. That's fouler.

Othello. Get me some poison, Iago, this night. I'll not expostulate with her, lest her body and beauty unprovide my mind again. This night, Iago! 209

Iago. Do it not with poison. Strangle her in her bed, even the bed she hath contaminated.

Othello. Good, good! The justice of it pleases. Very good!

Iago. And for Cassio, let me be his undertaker: you shall hear more by midnight. 214

Othello. Excellent good! [*A trumpet.*
 What trumpet is that same?

Iago. Something from Venice, sure.

Enter LODOVICO, DESDEMONA, *and* Attendants.
 'Tis Lodovico
Come from the Duke; and see, your wife is with him.

Lodovico. God save you, worthy general!

Othello. With all my heart, sir.

Lodovico. The Duke and senators of Venice greet you [*Gives him letter.*

Othello. I kiss the instrument of their pleasures.
 [*Opens the letter and reads.*

Desdemona. And what's the news, good cousin Lodovico?

Iago. I am very glad to see you, signior.
Welcome to Cyprus.

Lodovico. I thank you. How does Lieutenant Cassio?

Iago. Lives, sir.

Desdemona. Cousin, there's fall'n between him and my lord
An unkind breach; but you shall make all well.

Othello. Are you sure of that?

Desdemona. My lord?

Othello. [*reads*] 'This fail you not to do, as you will—'

Lodovico. He did not call; he's busy in the paper.
Is there division 'twixt thy lord and Cassio?

Desdemona. A most unhappy one. I would do much
T' atone them, for the love I bear to Cassio. 234

Othello. Fire and brimstone!

Desdemona. My lord?

Othello. Are you wise?

Desdemona. What, is he angry?

Lodovico. May be the letter moved him;
For, as I think, they do command him home,
Deputing Cassio in his government.

Desdemona. By my troth, I am glad on't.

Othello. Indeed?

Desdemona. My lord?

Othello. I am glad to see you mad.

201. "patent": license.

203. "messes": portions of food.

209. "unprovide": unsettle.

214. "undertaker": dispatcher.

234. "atone": reconcile.

OTHELLO

ACT IV SCENE I

"Get you away. . . . Hence, avaunt!" (259-61). Once more his speech becomes disjointed as he now reviles Desdemona, now addresses Lodovico, assuring him that he will obey the mandate and return to Venice. He appoints Cassio as his successor in Cyprus. Othello ends this speech with the coarse exclamation "Goats and Monkeys!" We have already explained the significance of the animal imagery underscoring the theme of carnality.

The general's conduct has now become inexcusable, to say the least, in an officer of the State especially. Lodovico pertinently asks, "Is this the noble Moor whom our full Senate/Call all in all sufficient?" (265-6), and in the three subsequent lines describes the virtues of Othello before the temptation. One must not forget that he is the author of his proper woe, his own downfall, however great that temptation was. He has permitted passion to "shake" him and to destroy his "solid virtue." In a word he has not survived the supreme test which the hero in high tragedy must undergo. If this were not so, we would have to conclude that Shakespeare's universe is not a moral one, since the great and good can be victimized so easily. Such is not true in this play or in any in the Shakespearean canon.

Iago presents himself as a man who is as much aggrieved as is Lodovico as the two conclude the scene with a brief bit of dialogue. The villain's "He is much changed" (269) is, for his despicable purpose, a most effective understatement. To the emissary, as to all others so far, he appears as honest and trustworthy.

Desdemona.   Why, sweet Othello —
Othello. Devil!   [*Strikes her.*
Desdemona. I have not deserved this.
Lodovico. My lord, this would not be believed in Venice,
Though I should swear I saw't. 'Tis very much.
Make her amends; she weeps.
Othello.   O devil, devil!
If that the earth could teem with woman's tears,   246
Each drop she falls would prove a crocodile.   247
Out of my sight!
Desdemona.   I will not stay to offend you. [*Going.*
Lodovico. Truly, an obedient lady.
I do beseech your lordship call her back.
Othello. Mistress!
Desdemona.   My lord?
Othello.   What would you with her, sir?
Lodovico. Who? I, my lord?
Othello. Ay! You did wish that I would make her turn.
Sir, she can turn, and turn, and yet go on
And turn again; and she can weep, sir, weep;
And she's obedient; as you say, obedient,
Very obedient. — Proceed you in your tears. —
Concerning this, sir — O well-painted passion! —   258
I am commanded home. — Get you away;
I'll send for you anon. — Sir, I obey the mandate
And will return to Venice. — Hence, avaunt!
           [*Exit* DESDEMONA.
Cassio shall have my place, And, sir, to-night
I do entreat that we may sup together.
You are welcome, sir, to Cyprus. — Goats and monkeys!   [*Exit.*
Lodovico. Is this the noble Moor whom our full Senate
Call all in all sufficient? Is this the nature
Whom passion could not shake? whose solid virtue
The shot of accident nor dart of chance
Could neither graze nor pierce?
Iago.   He is much changed.
Lodovico. Are his wits safe? Is he not light of brain?
Iago. He's that he is; I may not breathe my censure.
What he might be — if what he might he is not —
I would to heaven he were!
Lodovico.   What, strike his wife?
Iago. Faith, that was not so well; yet would I knew
That stroke would prove the worst!
Lodovico.   Is it his use?   275
Or did the letters work upon his blood
And new-create this fault?
Iago.   Alas, alas!
It is not honesty in me to speak
What I have seen and known. You shall observe him,
And his own courses will denote him so
That I may save my speech. Do but go after
And mark how he continues.
Lodovico. I am sorry that I am deceived in him.
           [*Exeunt.*

GONDOLA IN USE IN THE YEAR 1600.
From Franco. ob. cit.)

246. "teem": breed.

247. "crocodile": a reference to the hypocritical tears supposedly shed by crocodiles.

258. "passion": grief.

275. "use": custom.

Reference has been made to the "brothel" part of the preceding scene. But it is the present one which truly deserves that appellation. We first meet Othello questioning Emilia as regards the behavior of his wife and insinuating that Emilia must have observed Desdemona in compromising situations. But Iago's wife, who retrieves herself nobly after having obeyed her husband's instructions to get the handkerchief and later lying about her action, steadfastly vouches for the purity of the Moor's wife. Parenthetically it may be noted that when Othello demands particulars to support the alleged affair between Desdemona and Cassio Shakespeare again makes use of "double time," since the two had not been together often enough following the marriage to make any intrigue possible.

Othello curtly instructs Emilia to fetch his wife, whom he denounces as a "simple bawd" and a "subtle whore" (20-1). After first addressing her affectionately ("Pray, chuck, come hither") and dismissing Emilia. He puts his wife through a cruel ordeal of questions and accusations. He concludes that she is a whore and strumpet, ignoring her protestations of innocence.

Scene two.

(A ROOM IN THE CASTLE)

Enter OTHELLO *and* EMILIA.

Othello. You have seen nothing then?
Emilia. Nor ever heard, nor ever did suspect.
Othello. Yes, you have seen Cassio and she
    together.
Emilia. But then I saw no harm, and then I heard
Each syllable that breath made up between them.
Othello. What, did they never whisper?
Emilia.   Never, my lord.
Othello. Nor send you out o' th' way?
Emilia. Never.
Othello. To fetch her fan, her gloves, her mask, nor
    nothing?
Emilia. Never, my lord.
Othello. That's strange.
Emilia. I durst, my lord, to wager she is honest,
Lay down my soul at stake. If you think other,
Remove your thought; it doth abuse your bosom.
If any wretch have put this in your head,
Let heaven requite it with the serpent's curse!
For if she be not honest, chaste, and true,
There's no man happy; the purest of their wives
Is foul as slander.
Othello.   Bid her come hither. Go.
                    [*Exit* EMILIA.
She says enough; yet she's a simple bawd
That cannot say as much. This is a subtle whore,
A closet lock and key of villainous secrets;
And yet she'll kneel and pray; I have seen her do't.

Enter DESDEMONA *and* EMILIA.

Desdemona. My lord, what is your will?
Othello.   Pray, chuck, come hither.
Desdemona. What is your pleasure?
Othello.   Let me see your eyes.
Look in my face.
Desdemona.   What horrible fancy's this?
Othello. [*to Emilia*] Some of your function,
    mistress.
Leave procreants alone and shut the door;
Cough or cry hem if anybody come.
Your mystery, your mystery! Nay, dispatch!   30
                    [*Exit* EMILIA.
Desdemona. Upon my knees, what doth your speech
    import?
I understand a fury in your words,
But not the words
Othello. Why, what art thou?
Desdemona.   Your wife, my lord; your true
And loyal wife.

30. "mystery": trade.

OTHELLO

ACT IV SCENE II

The reader's attention is especially called to lines 71-81, wherein his egotism and morbid preoccupation with the theme of lechery is emphasized by his play upon the word *committed*. At the end of this distressing exhibition, the Moor calls for Emilia, identifying her as the keeper of Hell's Gate and giving her some money as if she were being paid for being a procuress. Yet there is some indication already of Othello's restoration as a tragic hero who invites understanding and some sympathy. It is not merely that he is so distraught at the loss of Desdemona that he cannot hold back his tears, but at line 47 he begins an eighteen-line speech, the larger part of which once more reveals the high-minded Moor who could voice great poetry. Notice, for example, the tacit reference to the afflictions of Job (47-53) and the broad range of imagery which expresses so clearly and movingly the turmoil in a man whose paradise is lost. The image of "a cistern of foul toads" (61), with its emphasis on gross sensuality, is followed by the startling vision of "Patience, thou rose-lipped cherubin" (63). Only such poetry replete with opposite figurative language could reveal so well the almost unbearable tension in Othello and the sudden change which has taken place in him.

Othello.   Come, swear it, damn thyself;
Lest, being like one of heaven, the devils themselves   36
Should fear to seize thee. Therefore be double-damned —
Swear thou art honest.
Desdemona.   Heaven doth truly know it.   38
Othello. Heaven truly knows that thou art false as hell.
Desdemona. To whom, my lord? With whom? How am I false?
Othello. Ah, Desdemon! away! away! away!
Desdemona. Alas the heavy day! Why do you weep?
Am I the motive of these tears, my lord?
If haply you my father do suspect
An instrument of this your calling back,   45
Lay not your blame on me. If you have lost him,
Why, I have lost him too.
Othello.   Had it pleased heaven
To try me with affliction, had they rained
All kinds of sores and shames on my bare head,
Steeped me in poverty to the very lips,
Given to captivity me and my utmost hopes,
I should have found in some place of my soul
A drop of patience. But, alas, to make me
A fixed figure for the time of scorn   54
To point his slow unmoving finger at!
Yet could I bear that too; well, very well,
But there where I have garnered up my heart,
Where either I must live or bear no life;
The fountain from the which my current runs
Or else dries up — to be discarded thence,
Or keep it as a cistern for foul toads
To knot and gender in — turn thy complexion there,   62
Patience, thou young and rose-lipped cherubin!
Ay, there look grim as hell!
Desdemona. I hope my noble lord esteems me honest.
Othello. O, ay; as summer flies are in the shambles,   66
That quicken even with blowing, O thou weed,   67
Who art so lovely fair, and smell'st so sweet,
That the sense aches at thee, would thou had'st ne'er been born!
Desdemona. Alas, what ignorant sin have I committed?
Othello. Was this fair paper, this most goodly book,
Made to write 'whore' upon? What committed?
Committed? O thou public commoner!   73
I should make very forges of my cheeks
That would to cinders burn up modesty,
Did I but speak thy deeds. What committed?
Heaven stops the nose at it, and the moon winks;   77
The bawdy wind, that kisses all it meets,
Is hushed within the hollow mine of earth
And will not hear it. What committed?
Impudent strumpet!
Desdemona.   By heaven, you do me wrong!
Othello. Are not you a strumpet?

36. "being . . . heaven": looking like an angel.

38. "honest": chaste.

45. "instrument": to be the cause.

54. "time of scorn": scorn of the age.

62. "turn . . . there": change thy color.

66. "shambles": slaughterhouse.

67. "quicken . . . blowing": come to life as soon as impregnated.

73. "commoner": harlot.

77. "winks": shuts her eyes.

After the Moor leaves, the kindly and greatly concerned Emilia endeavors to comfort her mistress. She is told in a few words that Othello is no longer Desdemona's "lord," that the young wife is too sorely distressed to find recourse in tears, and that she is at complete loss to explain this change in her husband's character. Desdemona has just one instruction, one that brings out strongly the pathos of her situation: let Emilia lay on her bed the wedding sheets. "Here's a change indeed," exclaimed Emilia (106) as she leaves to do her mistress's bidding.

Iago enters accompanied by his wife, and Desdemona turns to him for sympathy. She cannot bring herself to give him the details of what had just happened; it is Emilia who does so in her frank manner: "He called her a whore" (120). Iago appears nothing if not appalled by this information, and he makes further inquiry as to how all this came to happen. Of special interest is Emilia's speech (130-3) in which she expresses her conviction that "some eternal villain . . . Some busy and insinuating rogue, Some cogging, cozening slave," ambitious to obtain advancement has slandered Desdemona. The wary villain, once more knowing how dangerous his position is, quickly rejects this idea, stating that it is impossible that such a person could exist. Desdemona's lasting goodness is evident in her expression of hope that, if there is indeed such a villain, God may pardon him. But Emilia would have none of forgiveness under such circumstances; she hopes that whoever has "abused" the Moor will be whipped unmercifully. Iago orders her to lower her voice and then denounces her as a fool.

Desdemona.   No, as I am a Christian!
If to preserve this vessel for my lord
From any other foul unlawful touch
Be not to be a strumpet, I am none.
Othello. What, not a whore?
Desdemona.   No, as I shall be saved!
Othello. Is't possible?
Desdemona. O, heaven forgive us!
Othello.   I cry you mercy then.   88
I took you for that cunning whore of Venice
That married with Othello.—[*calling*] You, mistress,
That have the office opposite to Saint Peter
And keep the gate of hell!

Enter EMILIA.

                  You, you, ay, you!
We have done our course; there's money for your
      pains:
I pray you turn the key, and keep our counsel.
                                    [*Exit.*

Emilia. Alas, what does this gentleman conceive?
How do you, madam? How do you, my good lady?
Desdemona. Faith, half asleep.
Emilia. Good madam, what's the matter with my
      lord?
Desdemona. With who?
Emilia. Why, with my lord, madam.
Desdemona. Who is thy lord?
Emilia.   He that is yours, sweet lady.
Desdemona. I have none. Do not talk to me,
      Emilia.
I cannot weep; nor answer have I none
But what should go by water. Prithee to-night   104
Lay on my bed my wedding sheets, remember;
And call thy husband hither.
Emilia.   Here's a change indeed!
                                    [*Exit.*
Desdemona. 'Tis meet I should be used so, very
      meet.
How have I been behaved, that he might stick
The small'st opinion on my least misuse?   109

Enter IAGO *and* EMILIA.

Iago. What is your pleasure, madam? How is't
      with you?
Desdemona. I cannot tell. Those that do teach
      young babes
Do it with gentle means and easy tasks:
He might have chid me so; for, in good faith,
I am a child to chiding.
Iago.   What is the matter, lady?
Emilia. Alas, Iago, my lord hath so bewhored her,
Thrown such despite and heavy terms upon her
As true hearts cannot bear.
Desdemona. Am I that name, Iago?
Iago.   What name, fair lady?
Desdemona. Such as she says my lord did say I
      was.

88. "cry you mercy": beg your pardon.

104. "go by water": be rendered by tears.

109. "small'st opinion": least suspicion. "misuse": misconduct.

As further proof of her complete confidence in Iago, Desdemona pleads with him to tell her how she may win back the trust and love of Othello. The villain assures her that the Moor is troubled only by matters of state and thus is not himself. Desdemona and Emilia obey a summons to supper and leave the stage to Iago, who is immediately joined by Roderigo.

Emilia. He called her whore. A beggar in his drink
Could not have laid such terms upon his callet.   121
Iago. Why did he so?
Desdemona. I do not know; I am sure I am none
   such.
Iago. Do not weep, do not weep. Alas the day!
Emilia. Hath she forsook so many noble matches,
Her father and her country, all her friends,
To be called whore? Would it not make one weep?
Desdemona. It is my wretched fortune.
Iago.   Beshrew him for't!
How comes this trick upon him?
Desdemona.   Nay, heaven doth know. 129
Emilia. I will be hanged if some eternal villain,
Some busy and insinuating rogue,
Some cogging, cozening slave, to get some office,   132
Have not devised this slander. I'll be hanged else.
Iago. Fie, there is no such man! It is impossible.
Desdemona. If any such there be, heaven pardon
   him!
Emilia. A halter pardon him! and hell gnaw his
   bones!
Why should he call her whore? Who keeps her com-
   pany?
What place? what time? what form? what likeli-
   hood?
The Moor's abused by some most villainous knave,
Some base notorious knave, some scurvy fellow.
O heaven, that such companions thou'dst unfold,   141
And put in every honest hand a whip
To lash the rascals naked through the world
Even from the east to th' west!
Iago.   Speak within door.   144
Emilia. O, fie upon them! Some such squire he was
That turned your wit the seamy side without
And made you to suspect me with the Moor.
Iago. You are a fool. Go to.
Desdemona.   O good Iago,
What shall I do to win my lord again?
Good friend, go to him; for, by this light of heaven,
I know not how I lost him. Here I kneel:
If e'er my will did trespass 'gainst his love
Either in discourse of thought or actual deed,   153
Or that mine eyes, mine ears, or any sense
Delighted them in any other form,
Or that I do not yet, and ever did,
And ever will (though he do shake me off
To beggarly divorcement) love him dearly,
Comfort forswear me! Unkindness may do much;   159
And his unkindness may defeat my life,   160
But never taint my love. I cannot say 'whore.'
It doth abhor me now I speak the word;
To do the act that might th' addition earn
Not the world's mass of vanity could make me.
Iago. I pray you be content. 'Tis but his humor.
The business of the state does him offense,
(And he does chide with you.)
Desdemona. If 'twere no other —
Iago.   'Tis but so, I warrant.

121. "callet": whore.

129. "trick": foolish behavior.

132. "cogging, cozening": lying, cheating.

141. "companions": rogues.
"unfold": expose.

144. "within door": with restraint.

153. "discourse": course.

159. "comfort . . . me": happiness abandon me.
160. "defeat": destroy.

The young gull who, at Iago's insistence, has impoverished himself in the attempt to win the affection of Desdemona, is now in a state of revolt. He protests that the villain's "devices" have not helped him in the least. It is now abundantly clear that he believed that Iago had given his jewels to the Moor's wife; he now has a strong suspicion that he has been swindled. Roderigo is frank enough to call his solicitations "unlawful," and he states that he is ready to retire if Desdemona will return his jewels. Moreover, he threatens to seek satisfaction from Iago himself if he does not find redress. But the quick-thinking Iago subdues him for the time being. Again proving that he is the tactician who improvises as he goes along his path of villainy, he has, another plan which he assures Roderigo will work. The commission from Venice will appoint Cassio to Othello's place in Cyprus, according to Iago: let this man of "mettle," Roderigo, kill Cassio and then the Moor and Desdemona will have to remain in Cyprus. In order that the gull can carry out these actions Iago will arrange for Cassio to come out where Roderigo can attack him at an appropriately late hour of the night. Roderigo seems a bit dubious about all this, but he voices no protest when the villain assures him that he will be satisfied.

> [*Trumpets within.*
>
> Hark how these instruments summon you to supper.
> The messengers of Venice stay the meat: 170
> Go in, and weep not. All things shall be well.
>
> [*Exeunt* DESDEMONA *and* EMILIA.
>
> *Enter* RODERIGO.
>
> How now, Roderigo?
> *Roderigo.* I do not find that thou deal'st justly with me.
> *Iago.* What in the contrary?
> *Roderigo.* Every day thou daff'st me with some device, Iago, and rather, as it seems to me now, keep'st   175
> from me all conveniency than suppliest me with the   177
> least advantage of hope. I will indeed no longer
> endure it; nor am I yet persuaded to put up in peace
> what already I have foolishly suffered.
> *Iago.* Will you hear me, Roderigo?
> *Roderigo.* Faith, I have heard too much; for your
> words and performance are no kin together.
> *Iago.* You charge me most unjustly.
> *Roderigo.* With naught but truth. I have wasted
> myself out of means. The jewels you have had from
> me to deliver to Desdemona would half have corrupted a votarist. You have told me she hath received   188
> them, and returned me expectations and comforts of
> sudden respect and acquaintance; but I find none.   190
> *Iago.* Well, go to; very well.
> *Roderigo.* Very well! go to! I cannot go to, man;
> nor 'tis not very well. By this hand, I say 'tis very
> scurvy, and begin to find myself fopped in it.   194
> *Iago.* Very well.
> *Roderigo.* I tell you 'tis not very well. I will make
> myself known to Desdemona. If she will return me
> my jewels, I will give over my suit and repent my unlawful solicitation; if not, assure yourself I will seek
> satisfaction of you.
> *Iago.* You have said now.
> *Roderigo.* Ay, and said nothing but what I protest
> intendment of doing.
> *Iago.* Why, now I see there's mettle in thee; and
> even from this instant do build on thee a better opinion than ever before. Give me thy hand, Roderigo.
> Thou hast taken against me a most just exception;
> but yet I protest I have dealt most directly in thy
> affair.
> *Roderigo.* It hath not appeared.
> *Iago.* I grant indeed it hath not appeared, and your
> suspicion is not without wit and judgment. But,
> Roderigo, if thou hast that in thee indeed which I
> have greater reason to believe now than ever, I mean
> purpose, courage and valor, this night show it. If
> thou the next night following enjoy not Desdemona,
> take me from this world with treachery and devise
> engines for my life.   218
> *Roderigo.* Well, what is it? Is it within reason and
> compass?
> *Iago.* Sir, there is especial commission come from
> Venice to depute Cassio in Othello's place.

170. "stay the meat": wait to dine.

175. "thou . . . device": you put me off with some trick.

177. "conveniency": favorable opportunities.

188. "votarist": nun.

190. "sudden respect": speedy notice.

194. "fopped": duped.

218. "engines": plots.

Roderigo. Is that true? Why, then Othello and Desdemona return again to Venice.

Iago. O, no; he goes into Mauritania and takes away with him the fair Desdemona, unless his abode 226 be lingered here by some accident; wherein none 227 can be so determinate as the removing of Cassio. 228

Roderigo. How do you mean removing of him?

Iago. Why, by making him uncapable of Othello's place — knocking out his brains.

Roderigo. And that you would have me to do?

Iago. Ay, if you dare do yourself a profit and a right. He sups to-night with a harlotry, and thither will I go to him. He knows not yet of his honorable fortune. If you will watch his going thence, which I will fashion to fall out between twelve and one, you may take him at your pleasure. I will be near to second your attempt, and he shall fall between us. Come, stand not amazed at it, but go along with me. I will show you such a necessity in his death that you shall think yourself bound to put it on him. It is now high supper time, and the night grows to waste. About it!

Roderigo. I will hear further reason for this.

Iago. And you shall be satisfied. [*Exeunt.*

226-7. "abode . . . here": stay here be extended.
228. "determinate": effective.

Scene three.

(ANOTHER ROOM IN THE CASTLE)

Enter OTHELLO, LODOVICO, DESDEMONA, EMILIA, *and* Attendants.

Lodovico. I do beseech you, sir, trouble yourself no
    further.

Othello. O, pardon me; 'twill do me good to walk.

Lodovico. Madam, good night. I humbly thank
    your ladyship.

Desdemona. Your honor is most welcome.

Othello.   Will you walk, sir?
O, Desdemona —

Desdemona. My lord?

Othello. Get you to bed on th' instant; I will be returned forthwith. Dismiss your attendant there.
Look 't be done.

Desdemona. I will, my lord.

[*Exit* OTHELLO, *with* LODOVICO *and* Attendants.

Emilia. How goes it now? He looks gentler than he
    did.

Desdemona. He says he will return incontinent. 12
He hath commanded me to go to bed,
And bade me to dismiss you.

Emilia.   Dismiss me?

Desdemona. It was his bidding; therefore, good
    Emilia,
Give me my nightly wearing, and adieu.

12. "incontinent": at once.

Desdemona has recovered herself sufficiently and has shown her superior breeding by having presided as hostess at a dinner for Lodovico and other members of the commission from Venice. Othello expresses the desire to walk with Lodovico: " 'Twill do me good to walk" — an indication of his perturbed state. The Venetian thanks Desdemona for her hospitality and is graciously answered. Then Othello orders her to dismiss Emilia and to go to bed immediately. Dutifully the wife says that she will do so. Lodovico, the Moor, and the attendants depart.

OTHELLO

ACT IV SCENE III

Emilia, as concerned as ever, asks Desdemona how things are now going and expresses her belief that Othello "looks gentler than he did." Her mistress tells her how her husband had brusquely instructed her, whereupon the incensed Emilia exclaims that she wishes that she had never seen him. But Desdemona has no such wish, so strong is her rational love for the man of her choice. Yet she cannot finish her remarks on this subject. When Emilia tells her that the wedding sheets have been laid on the bed in accordance with Desdemona's wishes, the wife's reply is prophetic (23-25). It is apparent that she has a premonition of her own death, although, as the thought enters her mind, she endeavors to dismiss it as foolish. But she instructs Emilia to use the wedding sheets as a shroud for her if she should die before her waiting woman does. It is then that Desdemona provides the introduction for the mournful Willow Song, once sung by poor Barbary, her mother's maid, whose lover went mad and deserted her. Rather oddly, however, Desdemona then refers to Lodovico, praising him as a man who speaks well. Emilia is no less approving in her remarks. Exactly what Shakespeare intended here is hard to determine. It has been suggested that, for the moment, the young wife is comparing the foreigner Othello with the Venetians she had known. Or perhaps Desdemona's statement at line 35 should have been given to Emilia, whose relationship with Iago is anything but a romantic one and who would seem to have an eye for many members of the opposite sex.

The Willow Song was an old one, existing in versions and variants before Shakespeare incorporated it into his play. Not insignificant is line 51 which echoes, as it were, Desdemona's own statement in line 19-20. In the song, to be sure, it is the male lover who is false and the cause of the "poor soul's" sighing and weeping. The obvious point is that the mood perfectly reflects that of Desdemona.

The Moor's wife dismisses Emilia, but before the woman leaves both engage in a brief coliloquy on the subject of unfaithful wives. Desdemona is almost incredulous: can such creatures exist? The earthy Emilia replies that indeed they do, and she proceeds to make a kind of justification of a wife's infidelity when the stakes are high enough. Once more Desdemona cannot bring herself to believe that a wife could be false to her husband. In her last speech (83-102) Emilia now blames the husbands for their wives' behavior, insisting that the women have a right to avenge

We must not now displease him.

Emilia. I would you had never seen him!

Desdemona. So would I not. My love doth so approve him

That even his stubbornness, his checks, his frowns — 20
Prithee unpin me — have grace and favor in them.

Emilia. I have laid those sheets you bade me on the bed.

Desdemona. All's one. Good faith, how foolish are our minds!

If I do die before thee, prithee shroud me
In one of those same sheets.

Emilia.   Come, come! You talk.

Desdemona. My mother had a maid called Barbary.
She was in love; and he she loved proved mad   27
And did forsake her. She had a song of 'Willow';
An old thing 'twas; but it expressed her fortune,
And she died singing it. That song to-night
Will not go from my mind; I have much to do
But to go hang my head all at one side
And sing it like poor Barbary. Prithee dispatch.

Emilia. Shall I go fetch your nightgown?

Desdemona.   No, unpin me here.   34
This Lodovico is a proper man.

Emilia. A very handsome man.

Desdemona. He speaks well.

Emilia. I know a lady in Venice would have walked barefoot to Palestine for a touch of his nether lip.

Desdemona. [sings]
  'The poor soul sat sighing by a sycamore tree,
    Sing all a green willow;
  Her hand on her bosom, her head on her knee,
    Sing willow, willow, willow.
  The fresh streams ran by her and murmured her
      moans;
    Sing willow, willow, willow;
  Her salt tears fell from her, and soft'ned the
      stones' —

Lay by these.

  'Sing willow, willow, willow' —
Prithee hie thee: he'll come anon.   49
  'Sing all a green willow must be my garland.
  Let nobody blame him; his scorn I approve' —

Nay, that's not next. Hark! who is't that knocks?
Emilia. It is the wind.

Desdemona. [sings]
  'I called my love false love; but what said he
      then?
    Sing willow, willow, willow:
  If I court moe women, you'll couch with moe
      men.'

So, get thee gone; good night. Mine eyes do itch.
Doth that bode weeping?

20. "stubbornness": roughness.
"checks": rebukes.

27. "mad": wild.

34. "nightgown": dressing-gown.

49. "hie thee": hurry.

75

themselves upon wayward husbands. In effect, she argues that the double standard should be applicable to women since so many men adopt it to justify themselves. The intent of all this discourse is to keep to the fore the theme of infidelity. With a short prayer that she never be guilty of returning evil for evil, Desdemona says goodnight.

Emilia.   'Tis neither here nor there.

Desdemona. I have heard it said so. O, these men, these men!
Dost thou in conscience think — tell me, Emilia —
That there be women do abuse their husbands
In such gross kind?

Emilia.   There be some such, no question.

Desdemona. Wouldst thou do such a deed for all the world?

Emilia. Why, would not you?

Desdemona.   No, by this heavenly light!

Emilia. Nor I neither by this heavenly light.
I might do't as well i' th' dark.

Desdemona. Wouldst thou do such a deed for all the world?

Emilia. The world's a huge thing; it is a great price for a small vice.

Desdemona. Good troth, I think thou would'st not.

Emilia. By my troth, I think I should; and undo't when I had done it. Marry, I would not do such a thing for a joint-ring, nor for measures of lawn, nor for gowns, petticoats, nor caps, nor any petty exhibition; but, for all the whole world — 'Ud's pity! who would not make her husband a cuckold to make him a monarch? I should venture purgatory for't.

Desdemona. Beshrew me if I would do such a wrong
For the whole world.

Emilia. Why, the wrong is but a wrong i' th' world; and having the world for your labor, 'tis a wrong in your own world, and you might quickly make it right.

Desdemona. I do not think there is any such woman.

Emilia. Yes, a dozen; and as many to th' vantage as would store the world they played for.
But I do think it is their husbands' faults
If wives do fall. Say that they slack their duties
And pour our treasures into foreign laps;
Or else break out in peevish jealousies,
Throwing restraint upon us; or say they strike us,
Or scant our former having in despite —
Why, we have galls; and though we have some grace,
Yet have we some revenge. Let husbands know
Their wives have sense like them. They see, and smell,
And have their palates both for sweet and sour,
As husbands have. What is it that they do
When they change us for others? Is it sport?
I think it is. And doth affection breed it?
I think it doth. Is't frailty that thus errs?
It is so too. And have not we affections,
Desires for sport, and frailty, as men have?
Then let them use us well; else let them know,
The ills we do, their ills instruct us so.

Desdemona. Good night, good night. God me such usage send,
Not to pick bad from bad, but by bad mend!

[*Exeunt.*

72. "joint-ring": ring made in separable halves.
73. "exhibition": gift.

83. "to th' vantage": more, to boot.
84. "store": populate.

88. "peevish": silly.

90. "having": allowance.
91. "galls": spirits to resent.

103. "usage": habits.

72
73

83
84

88

90
91

103

In this scene which precedes the final one Shakespeare provides exciting physical action. Iago gives Roderigo final instructions for the attack on Cassio. As he says, the result of the action will make or mar them both (4), and he urges his dupe to be firm in his resolution. Roderigo himself is hardly a tower of determination and confidence, and the villain finds it necessary to re-assure him. The gull gives some evidence of a twinge of conscience but concludes that " 'Tis but a man gone" (10). At one side, Iago voices his thoughts: both Roderigo and Cassio are a source of danger to him; he stands to gain whichever one is slain. Of special interest are lines 18-20, wherein he acknowledges the fact that Cassio "hath a daily beauty in his life" that makes Iago himself "ugly." This passage provides the most convincing explantation of Iago's villainy, revealing as it does a man consumed by envy and egotism. It is true that Cassio's role has been sufficiently negative throughout the preceding action and that his affair with Bianca hardly redounds to his credit; but we must accept Iago's words at their face value and recognize that he sums up the public reputation of Cassio.

Cassio enters and is attacked by Roderigo. But the former lieutenant's coat of mail protects him. It is the gull who falls wounded and exclaiming that he is slain. At this crucial moment a desperate Iago darts from his place of hiding and severely wounds Cassio, who falls to the ground. Othello enters, convinced that the sounds of violence prove that Iago has kept his word to slay Cassio. He mistakes Roderigo for his former lieutenant, and he has high praise for "brave Iago" whom he believes to be "honest and just." Iago's prompt execution of revenge, convinces the Moor that he must do his duty. "Strumpet, I come," he exclaims (34) as he leaves to find the wife who he is now sure has betrayed him. He sees Iago's action as an act of justice, and he now sees himself as an executor of justice.

ACT FIVE, scene one.

(Cyprus. A Street)

Enter IAGO *and* RODERIGO.

Iago. Here, stand behind this bulk; straight will he come	1
Wear thy good rapier bare, and put it home.	
Quick, quick! Fear nothing; I'll be at thy elbow.	
It makes us, or it mars us — think on that,	
And fix most firm thy resolution.	
Roderigo. Be near at hand; I may miscarry in't.	
Iago. Here, at thy hand. Be bold, and take thy stand. [*Stands aside.*	
Roderigo. I have no great devotion to the deed,	
And yet he hath given me satisfying reasons.	
'Tis but a man gone. Forth my sword! He dies!	
Iago. I have rubbed this young quat almost to the sense,	11
And he grows angry. Now whether he kill Cassio,	
Or Cassio him, or each do kill the other,	
Every way makes my gain. Live Roderigo,	
He calls me to a restitution large	
Of gold and jewels that I bobbed from him	16
As gifts to Desdemona.	
It must not be. If Cassio do remain,	
He hath a daily beauty in his life	
That makes me ugly; and besides, the Moor	
May unfold me to him; there stand I in much peril.	
No, he must die. Be't so! I hear him coming.	

Enter CASSIO.

Roderigo. I know his gait. 'Tis he. Villain, thou diest!	
[*Makes a pass at* CASSIO.	
Cassio. That thrust had been mine enemy indeed	
But that my coat is better than thou know'st.	25
I will make proof of thine.	
[*Draws and wounds* RODERIGO.	
Roderigo. O, I am slain!	
IAGO *darts from concealment behind* CASSIO, *wounds him in the leg.* [*Exit.*	
Cassio. I am maimed for ever. Help, ho! Murder! murder! [*Exit.*	

Enter OTHELLO.

Othello. The voice of Cassio. Iago keeps his word.	
Roderigo. O, villain that I am!	
Othello. It is even so.	
Cassio. O, help, ho! light! a surgeon!	
Othello. 'Tis he. O brave Iago, honest and just,	
That hast such noble sense of thy friend's wrong!	
Thou teachest me. Minion, your dear lies dead,	33

1. "bulk": projecting shop front.

11. "quat": pimple.
"the sense": the quick.

16. "bobbed": cheated, swindled.

25. "coat": coat of mail worn under outer clothing.

33. "Minion": Mistress, or hussy, as here used.

Lodovico and his fellow emissary enter and hear Cassio's outcry and Roderigo's exclamation against the man who has mortally wounded him. In Lodovico's words, "It is a heavy night" (42). He leaves with his companion to find more help, while the pathetic gull bemoans the fact that he will bleed to death. Iago enters with a light, playing the familiar role of dissembler. It would seem that he just has been aroused as he makes his inquiry into matters. After a brief exchange with the wounded Cassio who recognizes Roderigo calling for help, Iago denounces Roderigo, his dupe, as a "murd'rous slave," stabs him and joins Lodovico and Gratiano. No one could appear more concerned or solicitous than Iago when he learns the nature of Cassio's leg wound. And so Bianca enters to find her "dear Cassio" fallen. Still the improviser, Iago states that he suspects the courtesan to have had a part in what has just happened. When the body of Roderigo is revealed in the light of a lantern, Iago appears more shaken than anyone else. He turns once more to Cassio, whose welfare seems to be his chief concern. Consistently it is Iago who has the proper maxim to climax his preceding remarks: "Nay, guiltiness will speak, Though tongues were out of use" (109-10).

And your unblest fate hies. Strumpet, I come.   34
Forth of my heart those charms, thine eyes, are
    blotted.
Thy bed, lust-stained, shall with lust's blood be
    spotted.   [*Exit.*

Enter LODOVICO *and* GRATIANO.

Cassio. What, ho? No watch? No passage? Murder!
    murder!   37
Gratiano. 'Tis some mischance. The cry is very
    direful.
Cassio. O, help!
Lodovico. Hark!
Roderigo. O wretched villain!
Lodovico. Two or three groan. It is a heavy night.   42
These may be counterfeits. Let's think't unsafe
To come in to the cry without more help.
Roderigo. Nobody come? Then shall I bleed to
    death.
Lodovico. Hark!

Enter IAGO, *with a light.*

Gratiano. Here's one comes in his shirt, with light
    and weapons.
Iago. Who's there? Whose noise is this that cries on
    murder?
Lodovico. We do not know.
Iago.   Did not you hear a cry?
Cassio. Here, here! For heaven's sake, help me!
Iago.   What's the matter?
Gratiano. This is Othello's ancient, as I take it.
Lodovico. The same indeed, a very valiant fellow.
Iago. What are you here that cry so grievously?
Cassio. Iago? O, I am spoiled, undone by villains!
Give me some help.
Iago. O me, lieutenant! What villains have done
    this?
Cassio. I think that one of them is hereabout
And cannot make away.
Iago.   O treacherous villains!
[*To* LODOVICO *and* GRATIANO] What are you there?
    Come in, and give some help.
Roderigo. O, help me here!
Cassio. That's one of them.
Iago.   O murd'rous slave! O villain!
                         [*Stabs* RODERIGO.
Roderigo. O damned Iago! O inhuman dog!
Iago. Kill men i' th' dark?—Where be these bloody
    thieves? —
How silent is this town! — Ho! murder! murder! —
What may you be? Are you of good or evil?
Lodovico. As you shall prove us, praise us.
Iago. Signior Lodovico?
Lodovico. He, sir.
Iago. I cry you mercy. Here's Cassio hurt by
    villains.
Gratiano. Cassio?

34. "hies": hurries on.

37. "passage": passers-by.

42. "heavy": dark.

Iago. How is it, brother?
Cassio. My leg is cut in two.
Iago.   Marry, heaven forbid!
Light, gentlemen. I'll bind it with my shirt.

Enter BIANCA.

Bianca. What is the matter, ho? Who is't that
    cried?
Iago. Who is't that cried?
Bianca. O my dear Cassio! my sweet Cassio!
O Cassio, Cassio, Cassio!
Iago. O notable strumpet! — Cassio, may you
    suspect
Who they should be that thus have mangled you?
Cassio. No.
Gratiano. I am sorry to find you thus. I have been
to seek you.
Iago. Lend me a garter. So. O for a chair   82
To bear him easily hence!
Bianca. Alas, he faints! O Cassio, Cassio, Cassio!
Iago. Gentlemen all, I do suspect this trash
To be a party in this injury. —
Patience awhile, good Cassio. — Come, come!
Lend me a light. Know we this face or no?
Alas, my friend and my dear countryman
Roderigo? No. — Yes, sure. — O heaven, Roderigo!
Gratiano. What, of Venice?
Iago. Even he, sir. Did you know him?
Gratiano.   Know him? Ay.
Iago. Signior Gratiano? I cry you gentle pardon.
These bloody accidents must excuse my manners
That so neglected you.
Gratiano.   I am glad to see you.
Iago. How do you, Cassio? — O, a chair, a chair!
Gratiano. Roderigo?
Iago. He, he, 'tis he! [*A chair brought in.*] O, that's
    well said; the chair.   98
Some good man bear him carefully from hence.
I'll fetch the general's surgeon. [*to* BIANCA] For you,
    mistress,
Save you your labor. — He that lies slain here, Cassio,
Was my dear friend. What malice was between
    you?
Cassio. None in the world; nor do I know the man.
Iago. [*to* BIANCA] What, look you pale· — O, bear
    him out o' th' air.
                 [CASSIO *and* RODERIGO *are borne off.*
Stay you, good gentlemen. — Look you pale, mis-
    tress? —
Do you perceive the gastness of her eye? —   106
Nay, if you stare, we shall hear more anon.
Behold her well; I pray you look upon her.
Do you see, gentlemen? Nay, guiltiness will speak,
Though tongues were out of use.

Enter EMILIA.

Emilia. 'Las, what's the matter? What's the matter
    husband?
Iago. Cassio hath here been set on in the dark

82. "chair": sedan chair.

98. "well said": well done.

106. "gastness": ghastliness, or terror.

ACT V SCENE I

Emilia arrives and learns of Cassio's wound and Roderigo's death, much to her genuine sorrow. As for Iago, he takes advantage of all this to voice sanctimonious words and to repeat his false suspicions regarding Bianca. It will be noted that Emilia still finds no reason to believe that her husband is anything but "honest." The villain sends his wife to inform Othello and Desdemona what has happened. Alone, he acknowledges the fact that his success or failure will be determined this very night — a clear indication that the resolution of the entire action is close at hand.

By Roderigo, and fellows that are scaped.
He's almost slain, and Roderigo dead.
Emilia. Alas, good gentlemen! alas, good Cassio!
Iago. This is the fruit of whoring. Prithee, Emilia,
Go know of Cassio where he supped to-night.
[*To* BIANCA] What, do you shake at that?
Bianca. He supped at my house; but I therefore
  shake not.
Iago. O, did he so? I charge you go with me.
Emilia. Fie, fie upon thee, strumpet!
Bianca. I am no strumpet, but of life as honest   122
As you that thus abuse me.
Emilia.   As I? Foh! fie upon thee!
Iago. Kind gentlemen, let's go see poor Cassio
  dressed.
[*To* BIANCA] Come, mistress, you must tell's another
  tale.
Emilia, run you to the citadel
And tell my lord and lady what hath happed.
                             [*Exit* EMILIA.
Will you go on afore?   [*Exeunt all but* IAGO.
          This is the night
That either makes me or fordoes me quite. [*Exit.* 129

122. "honest": chaste.

129. "fordoes": destroys.

Scene two.

(A BEDCHAMBER IN THE CASTLE)

DESDEMONA *asleep in her bed. Enter* OTHELLO *with a light.*

ACT V SCENE II

Othello, with a light, enters the bedroom where Desdemona lies asleep. His opening speech (1-15), following which he kisses his wife, reveals a Moor who has completely regained the stature of a tragic hero. In it are no references to strumpets and bawds, no employment of bestial images such as we found when he was racked with jealousy, "It is the cause, it is the cause, my soul." The cause, as the reference to "chaste stars" indicates, is that of unchastity. Yet Othello now sees himself, not as one seeking revenge for grievously injured pride, but as a man called upon to execute public justice. The very fact that he makes use of the term cause and avoids the explicit term for what he believes to be Desdemona's unforgivable offense is most revealing. No one can reasonably remain unmoved by the Moor's passionate conviction of righteousness or ignore the extent of his suffering, despite his monumental error. He is convinced that he is really being merciful in the performance of a deed which must be done. Thus he will not shed Desdemona's blood nor scar her physical beauty, no more than (as we learn a bit later) he would kill her soul. There is devastating irony in his use of the term light (7-10).

Othello. It is the cause, it is the cause, my soul.   1
Let me not name it to you, you chaste stars!
It is the cause. Yet I'll not shed her blood,
Nor scar that whiter skin of hers than snow,
And smooth as monumental alabaster.
Yet she must die, else she'll betray more men.
Put out the light, and then put out the light.
If I quench thee, thou flaming minister,   8
I can again thy former light restore,
Should I repent me; but once put out thy light,
Thou cunning'st pattern of excelling nature,
I know not where is that Promethean heat   12
That can thy light relume. When I have plucked the
  rose,   13
I cannot give it vital growth again;
It needs must wither, I'll smell thee on the tree.
                     [*He kisses her.*
O balmy breath, that dost almost persuade
Justice to break her sword! One more, one more!
Be thus when thou art dead, and I will kill thee,
And love thee after. One more, and this the last!
So sweet was ne'er so fatal. I must weep,
But they are cruel tears. This sorrow's heavenly;
It strikes where it doth love. She wakes.
Desdemona. Who's there? Othello?
Othello.   Ay, Desdemona.

1. "cause": cause of justice.

8. "minister": servant.

12. "Promethean heat": divine fire.

13. "relume": relight.

OTHELLO

ACT V SCENE II

for it is equated with reason — right reason, the angelic characteristic for which mankind should strive. As Othello kisses the sleeping Desdemona he is almost persuaded to spare her life. But he concludes that he must put her to death because hers is a deceptive beauty which masks corruption.

Desdemona awakes, and an agonizing discourse between husband and wife follows. The Moor urges her to pray for the forgiveness of any sin on her soul as the young wife becomes increasingly terrified. He mistakes the natural physical evidence of perturbation to be additional evidence of her guilt. Nor is he moved in the least by her insistence that she did not give the handkerchief to Cassio. It is notable that throughout this harrowing episode Othello's language is controlled and elevated. He voices "amen" to her prayer for divine mercy and addresses her as "Sweet soul." Nevertheless, he refuses to see her as anything but a "perjured woman" (63) who has forced him "to do/ A murder."

Desdemona. Will you come to bed, my lord?

Othello. Have you prayed to-night, Desdemon?

Desdemona.   Ay, my lord.

Othello. If you bethink yourself of any crime
Unreconciled as yet to heaven and grace,
Solicit for it straight.

Desdemona. Alack, my lord, what may you mean
  by that?

Othello. Well, do it, and be brief; I will walk by.
I would not kill thy unprepared spirit.
No, heaven forfend! I would not kill thy soul.   32

Desdemona. Talk you of killing?

Othello.   Ay, I do.

Desdemona.   Then heaven
Have mercy on me!

Othello.   Amen, with all my heart!

Desdemona. If you say so, I hope you will not
  kill me.

Othello. Hum!

Desdemona. And yet I fear you; for you are fatal
  then
When your eyes roll so. Why I should fear I know
  not,
Since guiltiness I know not; but yet I feel I fear.

Othello. Think on thy sins.

Desdemona.   They are loves I bear to you.

Othello. Ay, and for that thou diest.

Desdemona. That death's unnatural that kills for
  loving.
Alas, why gnaw you so your nether lip?
Some bloody passion shakes your very frame.
These are portents; but yet I hope, I hope,
They do not point on me.

Othello.   Peace and be still!

Desdemona. I will so. What's the matter?

Othello. That handkerchief which I so loved and
  gave thee
Thou gav'st to Cassio.

Desdemona.   No, by my life and soul!
Send for the man and ask him.

Othello.   Sweet soul, take heed,
Take heed of perjury; thou art on thy deathbed.

Desdemona. Ay, but not yet to die.

Othello.   Yes, presently.   52
Therefore confess thee freely of thy sin;
For to deny each article with oath
Cannot remove nor choke the strong conception   55
That I do groan withal. Thou art to die.

Desdemona. Then Lord have mercy on me!

Othello.   I say amen.

Desdemona. And have you mercy too! I never did
Offend you in my life; never loved Cassio   59
But with such general warranty of heaven
As I might love. I never gave him token.

Othello. By heaven, I saw my handkerchief in's
  hand!
O perjured woman! thou dost stone my heart,   63
And mak'st me call what I intend to do
A murder, which I thought a sacrifice.

32. "forfend": forbid.

52. "presently": at once.

55. "conception": belief.

59. "offend": wrong.

63. "stone my heart": make my heart turn to stone.

OTHELLO

ACT V SCENE II

Thus, for a moment, the motive of personal revenge rises again in the place of impersonal justice. As Desdemona continues to deny Othello's accusation, and particularly when she is told that Iago has slain Cassio and begins to weep the Moor can no longer delay. He smothers her as she cries out unto the Lord.

It is at this moment that Emilia arrives outside the door, crying loudly for Othello. But the Moor does not answer immediately. Still convinced that he is being merciful, he intends to be sure that his wife is dead. As he takes stock of the situation he does not know what to do next. The monstrosity of his deed seems to have become clear to him, and he exclaims: "My wife! my wife! what wife? I have no wife" (98). Significant are lines 100-102, in which he says that there should be now "a huge eclipse Of sun and moon" — that is, some evidence in the heavens that, because of Desdemona's fate, the very law of nature had been broken, the law, divine in origin, which makes possible order and tranquility in the universe. Little wonder that Othello finds all this to be "insupportable." Again Emilia calls out to the Moor, who had forgotten her very presence. Before he opens the door he closes the bedroom curtains so that Emilia will not see the smothered Desdemona.

I saw the handkerchief.

Desdemona.   He found it then.
I never gave it him. Send for him hither.
Let him confess a truth.

Othello.   He hath confessed.

Desdemona. What, my lord?

Othello. That he hath used thee.

Desdemona.   How? unlawfully?

Othello.   Ay.

Desdemona. He will not say so.

Othello.   No, his mouth is stopped.
Honest Iago hath ta'en order for't.   72

Desdemona. O, my fear interprets. What, is he dead?

Othello. Had all his hairs been lives, my great revenge
Had stomach for them all.

Desdemona. Alas, he is betrayed, and I undone!

Othello. Out, strumpet! Weep'st thou for him to my face?

Desdemona. O, banish me, my lord, but kill me not!

Othello. Down, strumpet!

Desdemona. Kill me to-morrow; let me live to-night!

Othello. Nay, an you strive —

Desdemona. But half an hour!

Othello.   Being done, there is no pause.

Desdemona. But while I say one prayer!

Othello.   It is too late.
          [*Smothers her.*

Desdemona. O Lord, Lord, Lord!

EMILIA *at the door.*

Emilia. [*calls within*] My lord, my lord! What, ho, my lord, my lord!

Othello. What noise is this? Not dead? not yet quite dead?
I that am cruel am yet merciful;
I would not have thee linger in thy pain.
So, so.

Emilia [*within*] What, ho! my lord, my lord!

Othello.   Who's there?

Emilia [*within*] O, good my lord, I would speak a word with you!

Othello. Yes, 'tis Emilia. — By and by. — She's dead. —
'Tis like she comes to speak of Cassio's death.
The noise was here. Ha! no more moving?
Still as the grave. — Shall she come in? Were't good? —
I think she stirs again. No. — What's best to do?
If she come in, she'll sure speak to my wife.
My wife! my wife! what wife? I have no wife.
O, insupportable! O heavy hour!
Methinks it should be now a huge eclipse
Of sun and moon, and that th' affrighted globe
Should yawn at alteration.

72. "ta'en order": taken measures.

Emilia reports that "foul murder" has been done. And now Othello learns to his dismay that Cassio survives and that it was Roderigo who had been slain. Desdemona revives to exclaim that she has been "falsely murdered." The startled Emilia demands an explanation; but Othello, to his discredit, pretends to be unaware that his wife had cried out. But the waiting woman, of course, recognized the voice as Desdemona's and she calls for help, then implores her mistress to speak. Once more the young wife proclaims her innocence and insists that no one but herself is to blame. Indeed she jeopardizes her very soul by telling a lie to protect the husband to whom she asks to be commended. With a farewell, Desdemona dies.

At first Othello denies any guilt for his wife's death but then, denouncing her as "a liar gone to burning hell," he admits that he killed her. His specific accusations against her follow, each refuted by the loyal Emilia. When he declares that Iago "knew it all," the villain's wife repeats "My husband? . . . my husband?" And Emilia learns that it was indeed Iago — "honest, honest Iago" who had viciously slandered the character of Desdemona. Without hesitation the waiting woman denounces her husband as "pernicious" and challenges Othello to do his worst to keep her still. Scorning him as a gull, a dolt, one "As ignorant as dirt" (164-5) she speaks for members of the audience and for those reading the play at this exciting point in the action. Fearlessly she ignore's the Moor's admonition to remain silent. She cries out for help and proclaims that Othello has slain Desdemona.

Emilia.   [*within*] I do beseech you   102
That I may speak with you, O good my lord!
Othello. I had forgot thee. O, come in, Emilia.
Soft, by and by. — Let me the curtains draw. —
         [*Closes the bed-curtains.*
Where art thou?   [*Opens the door.*

Enter EMILIA.

         What's the matter with thee now?
Emilia. O my good lord, yonder's foul murder
   done!
Othello. What? Now?
Emilia. But now, my lord.
Othello. It is the very error of the moon.   110
She comes more nearer earth than she was wont
And makes men mad.
Emilia. Cassio, my lord, hath killed a young Venetian.
Called Roderigo.
Othello.   Roderigo killed?
And Cassio killed?
Emilia.   No, Cassio is not killed.
Othello. Not Cassio killed? Then murder's out of
   tune,
And sweet revenge grows harsh.
Desdemona. O, falsely, falsely murdered!
Emilia.   O Lord! what cry is that?
Othello. That? What?
Emilia. Out and alas! that was my lady's voice.
Help! help, ho! help! O lady, speak again!
Sweet Desdemona! O sweet mistress, speak!
Desdemona. A guiltless death I die.
Emilia. O, who hath done this deed?
Desdemona. Nobody — I myself. Farewell.
Commend me to my kind lord. O, farewell!
         [*She dies.*
Othello. Why, how should she be murd'red?
Emilia.   Alas, who knows?
Othello. You heard her say herself, it was not I.
Emilia. She said so. I must needs report the
   truth.
Othello. She's like a liar gone to burning hell!
'Twas I that killed her.
Emilia.   O, the more angel she,
And you the blacker devil!
Othello. She turned to folly, and she was a whore.
Emilia. Thou dost belie her, and thou art a devil.
Othello. She was false as water.
Emilia.   Thou art rash as fire to say
That she was false. O, she was heavenly true!
Othello. Cassio did top her. Ask thy husband else.
O, I were damned beneath all depth in hell
But that I did proceed upon just grounds
To this extremity. Thy husband knew it all.
Emilia. My husband?
Othello. Thy husband.
Emilia. That she was false to wedlock?
Othello. Ay, with Cassio. Nay, had she been true,

102. "yawn": open, as in an earthquake.

110. "error": wandering.

If heaven would make me such another world
Of one entire and perfect chrysolite,   146
I'ld not have sold her for it.

Emilia. My husband?

Othello.   Ay, 'twas he that told me first.
An honest man he is, and hates the slime
That sticks on filthy deeds.

Emilia.   My husband?

Othello. What needs this iterance? Woman, I say
    thy husband.

Emilia. O mistress, villainy hath made mocks with
    love!
My husband say that she was false?

Othello.   He, woman.
I say, thy husband. Dost understand the word?
My friend, thy husband; honest, honest Iago.

Emilia. If he say so, may his pernicious soul
Rot half a grain a day! he lies to th' heart.
She was too fond of her most filthy bargain.

Othello. Ha!

Emilia. Do thy worst.
This deed of thine is no more worthy heaven
Than thou wast worthy her.

Othello.   Peace, you were best.

Emilia. Thou hast not half the power to do me
    harm
As I have to be hurt. O gull! O dolt!   164
As ignorant as dirt! thou hast done a deed —
I care not for thy sword; I'll make thee known,
Though I lost twenty lives. Help! help! O, help!
The Moor hath killed my mistress! Murder! murder!

Enter MONTANO, GRATIANO, IAGO, *and others.*

Montano. What is the matter? How now, general?

Emilia. O, are you come, Iago? You have done
    well,
That men must lay their murders on your neck.

Gratiano. What is the matter?

Emilia. Disprove this villain, if thou be'st a man.
He says thou told'st him that his wife was false.
I know thou did'st not; thou'rt not such a villain.
Speak, for my heart is full.

Iago. I told him what I thought, and told no more
Than what he found himself was apt and true.

Emilia. But did you ever tell him she was false?

Iago. I did.

Emilia. You told a lie, an odious damned lie!
Upon my soul, a lie! a wicked lie!
She false with Cassio? Did you say with Cassio?

Iago. With Cassio, mistress. Go to, charm your
    tongue.   184

Emilia. I will not charm my tongue; I am bound
    to speak:
My mistress here lies murdered in her bed —

All. O heavens forfend!

Emilia. And your reports have set the murder on.

Othello. Nay, stare not, masters. It is true indeed.

Gratiano. 'Tis a strange truth.

146. "chrysolite": a precious stone.

164. "to be hurt": to endure hurt.

184. "charm": cast a spell on.

Montano, Gratiano, Iago and others enter. For the moment ignoring Montano's demand to know what has happened, Emilia excoriates her husband as one who has "done well" to be deserved to be called a murderer. She challenges him to disprove what Othello has told her. Yet she expresses what must be no more than a faint hope that her husband is "not such a villain" (175). In response to her pointed questions, Iago concedes that he had reported Desdemona to be false and insists that he told no more than what Othello found to be "apt and true" (178). The soul of courage, Emilia ignores her husband's command to be quiet and to go home. Again denouncing Iago and imploring the others to hear her, she prophetically states that she will never go home (198). All this becomes unbearable for the Moor, who falls upon the bed, only to be upbraided once more by Iago's wife. He rises to face Gratiano, uncle to Desdemona, and to admit that he has smothered her. "Poor Desdemona!" Gratiano exclaims and finds comfort only in the fact that Brabantio has not survived to endure this latest great cause for sorrow. We learn that his daughter's elopement had indeed broken his heart and that grief had killed him.

OTHELLO

ACT V SCENE II

Othello voices his sympathy but insists that, as Iago "knows," Desdemona had committed "the act of shame" with Cassio " a thousand times" (212-13) — another example of "double time" in the play. Further he makes reference to what he believes to be ocular proof, the handkerchief. At the mention of this, Emilia cries out once more, appealing to God: murder will out; no one will now silence her. Again she refuses to obey her husband's command to leave, and he draws his sword and threatens her, to the astonishment of Gratiano. Emilia tells how she had found the handkerchief and given it to her husband. She is denounced by Iago as a "Villainous whore!" (230) and a liar. Thus has begun the counter-discovery for Othello; his eyes are beginning at last to be opened to the truth. In his torment he asks if heaven itself cannot spare one thunderbolt for Iago. As he runs at the villain, Montano disarms him. Iago stabs Emilia, who falls to the floor as her husband flees. Montano gives the order for the villain's apprehension. All leave except the dying Emilia and the Moor, who can only berate himself. Aware that she is near death, the waiting woman recalls Desdemona's prophetic Willow Song, a bit of which she sings. She reaffirms the innocence of her mistress just before she dies and concludes: "She loved thee cruel Moor" . . . (250).

Montano. O monstrous act!

Emilia.   Villainy, villainy, villainy!
I think upon't — I think I smell't! — O villainy!
I thought so then. — I'll kill myself for grief. —   193
O villainy, villainy!

  Iago. What, are you mad? I charge you get you
    home.

  Emilia. Good gentlemen, let me have leave to
    speak.
'Tis proper I obey him, but not now.
Perchance, Iago, I will ne'er go home.

  Othello. O! O! O!   [*Falls on the bed.*

  Emilia.   Nay, lay thee down and roar!
For thou hast killed the sweetest innocent
That e'er did lift up eye.

  Othello.   O, she was foul!   [*Rises.*
I scarce did know you, uncle. There lies your niece,
Whose breath, indeed, these hands have newly
    stopped.
I know this act shows horrible and grim.   204

  Gratiano. Poor Desdemon! I am glad thy father's
    dead.
Thy match was mortal to him, and pure grief
Shore his old thread in twain. Did he live now,
This sight would make him do a desperate turn;   208
Yea, curse his better angel from his side,
And fall to reprobation.   210

  Othello. 'Tis pitiful; but yet Iago knows
That she with Cassio hath the act of shame
A thousand times committed. Cassio confessed it;
And she did gratify his amorous works   214
With that recognizance and pledge of love   215
Which I first gave her. I saw it in his hand.
It was a handkerchief, an antique token
My father gave my mother.

  Emilia. O God! O heavenly God!

  Iago. Zounds, hold your peace!

  Emilia.   'Twill out, 'twill out! I peace?
No, I will speak as liberal as the north.   221
Let heaven and men and devils, let them all,
All, all, cry shame against me, yet I'll speak.

  Iago. Be wise, and get you home.

  Emilia.   I will not.

        [IAGO *draws and threatens* EMILIA.

  Gratiano.   Fie!
Your sword upon a woman?

  Emilia. O thou dull Moor, that handkerchief thou
    speak'st of
I found by fortune, and did give my husband;
For often with a solemn earnestness —
More than indeed belonged to such a trifle —
He begged of me to steal't.

  Iago.   Villainous whore!

  Emilia. She give it Cassio? No, alas, I found it,
And I did give't my husband.

  Iago.   Filth, thou liest!

  Emilia. By heaven, I do not, I do not, gentlemen.
O murd'rous coxcomb! what should such a fool
Do with so good a wife?

193. "I thought so then": refers to IV, ii.130-33.

204. "shows": seems.

208. "turn": act.

210. "reprobation": rejection by God.

214. "gratify": reward.
215. "recognizance": token.

221. "liberal as the north": freely as the north wind blows.

OTHELLO

Othello finds another of his prized weapons, a sword of Spain, and announces that he "must come forth" (255). To Gratiano, who appears at this moment, he makes reference to the sword and how he has used it in the past. Now, he continues, it avails him nothing and Gratiano has nothing to fear. He sees himself as a lost soul ("Where should Othello go?") and as an "accursed slave" who deserves the worst of punishment.

Lodovico, Montano, Iago (as a prisoner) and officers enter; Cassio, in a chair, is brought in. The moment of complete revelation is at hand. Othello wounds Iago and is disarmed by order of Lodovico. Nor does the Moor protest: the man for whom death would now be a relief would not have his arch-enemy find such solace. When Cassio simply states that he had never given the Moor reason to distrust him, the crushed general readily accepts his word and asks for his pardon. Thus Othello has learned that he had been ensnared body and soul by "that demi-devil" Iago, who refuses to say anything about his villainy (304-5). Lodovico produces letters, one of which tells of Roderigo's plan to slay Cassio, the other the dupe's denunciation of Iago. All the details of how Cassio obtained the handkerchief are disclosed. The Moor can only bewail the fact that he had been such a fool.

Othello.   Are there no stones in heaven 235
But what serves for the thunder? Precious villain!
THE MOOR *runs at* IAGO, *but is disarmed by* MONTANO.
    IAGO *kills his wife.*
Gratiano. The woman falls. Sure he hath killed
 his wife.
Emilia. Ay, ay. O, lay me by my mistress' side.
          [*Exit* IAGO.
Gratiano. He's gone, but his wife's killed.
Montano. 'Tis a notorious villain. Take you this
 weapon. 240
Which I have here recovered from the Moor.
Come, guard the door without. Let him not pass,
But kill him rather. I'll after that same villain,
For 'tis a damned slave.

  [*Exit* MONTANO, *with all but* OTHELLO *and* EMILIA.

Othello.   I am not valiant neither;
But every puny whipster gets my sword. 245
But why should honor outlive honesty?
Let it go all.
Emilia. What did thy song bode, lady?
Hark, canst thou hear me? I will play the swan,
And die in music. [*Sings*] 'Willow, willow, willow.'
Moor, she was chaste. She loved thee, cruel Moor:
So come my soul to bliss as I speak true.
So speaking as I think, I die, I die. [*She dies.*
Othello. I have another weapon in this chamber;
It is a sword of Spain, the Isebrook's temper. 254
O, here it is. — Uncle, I must come forth.
Gratiano. [*within*] If thou attempt it, it will cost
 thee dear.
Thou hast no weapon, and perforce must suffer.
Othello. Look in upon me then and speak with me,
Or, naked as I am, I will assault thee. 259

    Enter GRATIANO.

Gratiano. What is the matter?
Othello.   Behold, I have a weapon;
A better never did itself sustain
Upon a soldier's thigh. I have seen the day
That with this little arm and this good sword
I have made my way through more impediments
Than twenty times your stop. But O vain boast! 265
Who can control his fate? 'Tis not so now.
Be not afraid, though you do see me weaponed.
Here is my journey's end, here is my butt, 268
And very seamark of my utmost sail. 269
Do you go back dismayed? 'Tis a lost fear. 270
Man but a rush against Othello's breast, 271
And he retires. Where should Othello go?
Now, how dost thou look now? O ill-starred wench!
Pale as thy smock! When we shall meet at compt, 274
This look of thine will hurl my soul from heaven,
And fiends will snatch at it. Cold, cold, my girl?
Even like thy chastity.
O cursed, cursed slave! Whip me, ye devils,
From the possession of this heavenly sight!

235. "stones": bolts such as used for thunderbolts.

240. "notorious": notable.

245. "whipster": term of contempt.

254. "Isebrook's temper": tempered in Innsbruck, which was noted for its superior steel.

259. "naked": unarmed.

265. "stop": power to stop.

268. "butt": goal.
269. "seamark": beacon, destination.
270. "lost": wasted.
271. "man but a rush": wield only a reed.

274. "compt": accounting on Judgment Day.

Blow me about in winds! roast me in sulphur!
Wash me in steep-down gulfs of liquid fire!
O Desdemona, Desdemona! dead!
O! O! O!

     Enter LODOVICO, MONTANO, IAGO *as prisoner,*
      and Officers; CASSIO *in a chair.*

Lodovico. Where is this rash and most unfortunate
    man?
Othello. That's he that was Othello. Here I am.
Lodovico. Where is that viper? Bring the villain
    forth.
Othello. I look down towards his feet — but that's
    a fable.   287
If that thou be'st a devil, I cannot kill thee.
                               [*Wounds* IAGO.
Lodovico. Wrench his sword from him.
                      [OTHELLO *is disarmed.*
Iago.   I bleed, sir, but not killed.
Othello. I am not sorry neither. I'd have thee live;
For in my sense, 'tis happiness to die.
Lodovico. O thou Othello that wert once so good,
Fall'n in the practice of a damned slave,   293
What shall be said to thee?
Othello.   Why, anything:
An honorable murderer, if you will;
For naught did I in hate, but all in honor.
Lodovico. This wretch hath part confessed his
    villainy.
Did you and he consent in Cassio's death?   298
Othello. Ay.
Cassio. Dear general, I never gave you cause.
Othello. I do believe it, and I ask your pardon.
Will you, I pray, demand that demi-devil
Why he hath thus ensnared my soul and body?
Iago. Demand me nothing. What you know, you
    know.
From this time forth I never will speak word.
Lodovico. What, not to pray?
Gratiano.   Torments will ope your lips.
Othello. Well, thou dost best.
Lodovico. Sir, you shall understand what hath be-
    fall'n,
Which, as I think, you know not. Here is a letter
Found in the pocket of the slain Roderigo;
And here another. The one of them imports
The death of Cassio to be undertook
By Roderigo.
Othello. O villain!
Cassio.   Most heathenish and most gross!
Lodovico. Now here's another discontented paper
Found in his pocket too; and this, it seems,
Roderigo meant t' have sent this damned villain;
But that, belike, Iago in the nick   318
Came in and satisfied him.
Othello.   O thou pernicious caitiff! —
How came you, Cassio, by that handkerchief
That was my wife's?
Cassio.   I found it in my chamber;

287. "I . . . feet": i.e., to see if they are
cloven as the devil's were thought
to be.

293. "practice": plot.

298. "consent in": agree upon.

318. "nick": nick of time.

It is quite appropriate that Iago's life should be spared at this time, for this is Othello's play and the death of the tragic hero must be the ultimate resolution of the action. Nothing must detract from it. It is enough for us to learn, from Lodovico's words (335-6), that torment will force the villain to tell all the details of his actions before he is sentenced as the master-criminal who had poisoned the Moor's mind and caused such general misery.

Before Othello can be led away, he speaks his final lines (339-57). Now unmistakably he has recovered his essential nobility and that gift of impressive language which he had commanded so well prior to the temptation. At the start he reminds his listeners of his past service to the State and pleads that his story be reported accurately so that all will know him not as a barbarous foreigner but as one who had "loved not wisely but too well"; one who had been worked upon and had become "perplexed in the extreme" and thus driven to act in such a cruel manner. No one will overlook or forget the magnificent simile that he uses when he compares himself to the "base Judean" who threw away the most valuable pearl in the world. Relentless in his self-reproach, he tacitly compares himself to "a malignant and turbaned Turk." He stabs himself, an act of attempted atonement — a "bloody period," in Lodovico's words, to all that has happened. Othello sees himself as executing poetic justice upon himself for the slaying of Desdemona, thus his final two lines are spoken just before he dies.

And he himself confessed but even now
That there he dropped it for a special purpose
Which wrought to his desire.
Othello.   O fool! fool!! fool!
Cassio. There is besides in Roderigo's letter,
How he upbraids Iago that he made him
Brave me upon the watch; whereon it came
That I was cast; and even but now he spake,   328
After long seeming dead — Iago hurt him,
Iago set him on.
Lodovico. You must forsake this room and go
    with us.
Your power and your command is taken off,
And Cassio rules in Cyprus. For this slave,
If there be any cunning cruelty
That can torment him much and hold him long,
It shall be his. You shall close prisoner rest
Till that the nature of your fault be known
To the Venetian state. Come, bring away.
Othello. Soft you! a word or two before you go.
I have done the state some service, and they know 't.
No more of that. I pray you, in your letters,
When you shall these unlucky deeds relate,
Speak of me as I am. Nothing extenuate,
Nor set down aught in malice. Then must you speak
Of one that loved not wisely, but too well;
Of one not easily jealous, but, being wrought,
Perplexed in the extreme; of one whose hand,   347
Like the base Judean, threw a pearl away   348
Richer than all his tribe; of one whose subdued
    eyes,   349
Albeit unused to the melting mood,
Drop tears as fast as the Arabian trees
Their med'cinable gum. Set you down this.
And say besides that in Aleppo once,
Where a malignant and turbaned Turk
Beat a Venetian and traduced the state,
I took by th' throat the circumcised dog
And smote him — thus   [*He stabs himself.*
Lodovico. O bloody period!
Gratiano.   All that 's spoke is marred. 358
Othello. I kissed thee ere I killed thee. No way but
    this,
Killing myself, to die upon a kiss.
             [*He falls upon the bed and dies.*
Cassio. This did I fear, but thought he had no
    weapon;
For he was great of heart.
Lodovico.   [*to* IAGO] O Spartan dog,   362
More fell than anguish, hunger, or the sea!   363
Look on the tragic loading of this bed.
This is thy work. The object poisons sight;
Let it be hid. Gratiano, keep the house,   366
And seize upon the fortunes of the Moor,   367
For they succeed on you. To you, lord governor,
Remains the censure of this hellish villain,   369
The time, the place, the torture. O, enforce it!
Myself will straight aboard, and to the state
This heavy act with heavy heart relate.   [*Exeunt.*

328. "cast": dismissed.

347. "perplexed": distraught.

348. "Judean" possible reference to Judas Iscariot.

349. "subdued": conquered by grief.

358. "period": ending.

362. "Spartan dog": bloodhound.

363. "fell": cruel.

366. "Let it be hid": i.e., let the curtains be drawn.

367. "seize upon": confiscate.

369. "censure": judicial sentence.

Bibliography

EDITIONS

A New Variorum Edition of Shakespeare, ed. Horace H. Furness. New York: J. B. Lippincott, 1871———. (Reprints by The American Scholar and Dover Publications.) Each play is dealt with in a separate volume of monumental scholarship.

The Yale Shakespeare, ed. Helge Kökeritz and Charles T. Prouty. New Haven: Yale University Press, 1955———. A multi-volume edition founded on modern scholarship.

COMMENTARY AND CRITICISM

Bentley, G. E. *Shakespeare and His Theatre.* Lincoln: University of Nebraska Press, 1964 (paperback). Illuminating discussion of the actual conditions under which, and for which, Shakespeare wrote.

Bradley, A. C. *Shakespearean Tragedy: Lectures on Hamlet, Othello, King Lear, Macbeth.* New York: Macmillan, 1904. (Paperback ed.; New York: Meridian Books, 1955.) A classic examination of the great tragedies.

Chambers, Edmund K. *William Shakespeare: A Study of Facts and Problems*, 2 vols. Oxford: Clarendon Press, 1930. Indispensable source for bibliographical and historical information.

Chute, Marchette. *Shakespeare of London.* New York: E. P. Dutton, 1949. A vivid account of Shakespeare's career in the dynamic Elizabethan metropolis.

Granville-Barker, Harley. *Prefaces to Shakespeare.* London: Sidgwick & Jackson, 1927-47. (2 vols.; Princeton: Princeton University Press, 1947.) Stimulating studies of ten plays by a scholarly man of the theater.

Harbage, Alfred. *Shakespeare's Audience.* New York: Columbia University Press, 1941. Revealing approach to Shakespeare as a practical man of the theater.

Knight, Wilson. *The Wheel of Fire.* London: Oxford University Press, 1930. Stresses the power of intuition to capture the total poetic experience of Shakespeare's work.

Spurgeon, Caroline. *Shakespeare's Imagery and What It Tells Us.* Cambridge: Cambridge University Press, 1935. A psychological study of the playwright's imagery as a means to understanding the man himself.